THE
WEDDING
BOOK

"The Contract" from *Marriage à la Mode* by William Hogarth

THE WEDDING BOOK

Alternative Ways to Celebrate Marriage

*Howard Kirschenbaum and
Rockwell Stensrud*

A CROSSROAD BOOK
THE SEABURY PRESS
NEW YORK

The Seabury Press
815 Second Avenue
New York, N.Y. 10017

ACKNOWLEDGMENTS

See page 279, which constitutes an extension
of this copyright page.

Library of Congress Cataloging in Publication Data

Kirschenbaum, Howard.
　The wedding book.

　"A Crossroad book."
　　1. Weddings.　2. Marriage customs and rites.
I. Stensrud, Rockwell, joint author.　II. Title.
HQ745.K57　　　395'.22　　　73-17901
ISBN 0-8164-0257-4
ISBN 0-8164-2090-4 (pbk.)

FOR BARB, AND
JANET AND ROCK

Contents

THE
WEDDING
BOOK

1
Jan and
Ed

"IT HAS BEEN WRITTEN:
'A LOAF OF BREAD,
A JUG OF WINE' (some steak, chicken, potato salad,
   chips, beer, etc.) 'AND THOU'
is about all that's truly necessary to . . . (check below)

_____ START THE FUTURE

_____ KISS AND MAKE UP

_____ RENEW OLD, REVIEW NEW

_____ "REMEMBER WHEN" AWHILE

_____ HAVE SOME FUN

_____ GET SOME FREE EATS

_____ JUST LET IT BEEEEEE."

It was typical of Jan and Ed to take a quote
from the _Rubaiyat of Omar Khayyam_ and expand it
into a wedding invitation. Some people may have been
taken by surprise, but anyone who knew them well
would have smiled; doing a common thing in a unique
way was part of what made them special. Their invitation had been run off on a duplicating machine,

saving time and money and enabling them to do the invitation themselves.

Jan and Ed had lived together for two years before they decided to get married. At first they hadn't thought of marriage as the most important part of their relationship, and both had wanted to see if they could live together happily before making a formal commitment. During those two years they often talked about what marriage meant to them—the hopes, the expectations, and the realities. When they did decide to get married, they had a good idea of what each one wanted in the years ahead.

After the invitations were delivered, friends called to congratulate them. Few expressed surprise that the couple had decided to depart from traditional customs. Jan and Ed were teachers working in a black inner-city school. Both were white. They were committed to social change through education and community action groups. Both wanted to make society more responsive to people's needs, and they believed in searching for new ways for people to live happy lives. They wanted their wedding to reflect these values.

When Jan and Ed discussed alternatives to a church ceremony, they decided to rent a private park outside the city for the site of their wedding. The park had a picnic area, forests, a waterfall, and running streams. Across one of the footbridges was a secluded spot surrounded by tall trees. This was the site they chose for the ceremony. Nearer to the parking area was a long field with tables and barbecue pits that would be fine for the reception.

They prepared their own ceremony and asked a friend who was a minister to officiate. The only part still left to plan was the reception. Ed called several friends and asked them to help out. (If it had been a traditional wedding, he would have asked them to be groomsmen.) One offered to be the cook, another the bartender, and a third said he would help serve the meal. Other guests wanted to bring salads and desserts for the feast; Jan and Ed figured out how much of which dish each person should bring. After many telephone calls and menu revisions, the reception plans were complete. All that remained to do after that was order the steaks.

The ceremony was announced for three o'clock on a Saturday afternoon in June. The cook and the bartender arrived early and began setting up; as other guests came, they helped set the tables and arrange the food. Jan and Ed had encouraged them to come early so everyone could get to know one another before the ceremony. Many of the friends and relatives sat talking in small groups. Some strummed on guitars and sang. A few stood around giving advice to the cook and bartender. Others tossed a Frisbee back and forth or sat by the waterfall or went walking in the woods. Jan and Ed took an active part, moving from group to group, chatting with friends and relatives— some they hadn't seen in months or years. The informality made it easier to strike up conversation with a stranger, something that is very difficult in a church or a reception hall where everyone is seated in rows or at tables with people they already know. In the park the atmosphere was relaxed and the guests moved easily among groups. One of Jan's uncles, an illustrator, walked from group to group sketching the guests. As his gift to Jan and Ed, he gave the sketches he had made to the guests as mementos.

A few of the guests, especially older relatives, had been apprehensive about attending an unusual wedding. They hadn't known what to expect—or what to wear. Jan and Ed told everyone to wear whatever was comfortable, and the result was an array of styles —pants suits, shorts, slacks and sport shirts, skirts, and jeans. No one seemed or felt out of place, and the variety of styles and colors suggested a festive, happy mood.

As three o'clock approached, the guests crossed over the bridge to the site of the ceremony. Ed handed everyone a sheet of poems and readings and asked that everyone be silent. Just crossing the bridge seemed to change the tone from gaiety to a respectful, expectant silence.

Jan and Ed stood in front with their families and the minister. Their backs were to the waterfall. Several semicircles of guests settled themselves on blankets or stood facing the wedding party. The minister stood in the center of the line, with Jan on one side and Ed on the other. When everyone was comfortable, the minister began to lead the service that Jan and Ed had prepared, writing much of it themselves.

We are gathered here today to join together this man and this woman in marriage—an estate instituted in love, occasioned by joy, and honored and renewed by

each man and woman who pledge themselves to one another. It is, therefore, not by any to be entered into unadvisedly or lightly, but with discretion and reverence
for its responsibility, as well as with praise and delight
for its inexpressible gifts.

This celebration is the outward token of an inward
union of hearts, which the Church may bless and the
State make legal, but which neither State nor Church
can create or annul, a union created by loving purpose
and kept by abiding will. It is for us merely to acknowledge the true marriage which already dwells in these
two hearts.

Then the minister asked, "Would anyone in this
gathering like to share his or her thoughts with us?"
After a short pause, a fellow teacher of Jan and Ed
spoke. "I'd like to say now what the two of you
have meant to me during the past two years we've
worked together and shared parts of our lives with
each other. So many times when I was feeling confused,
or like giving up, I'd see both of you struggling on and
keeping your good humor and supporting me when I
needed it. Your example meant more to me than you'll
ever know. And for that I'd like to say thanks."

Then a married couple in the group sang a Bul-
garian wedding chant, and another guest played his
guitar and sang a song in which he invited anyone who
wished to join in on the chorus.

And today while the blossoms still cling to the vine,
I'll taste your strawberries, I'll drink your sweet wine.

A million tomorrows shall all pass away
Ere I forget all the joys that were ours today.

Oh, I'll be a dandy and I'll be a rover,
You'll know who I am by the songs that I sing.
I'll feast at your table, I'll sleep in your clover,
Who cares what tomorrow shall bring? (And
    today . . .)

I can't be contented with yesterday's glories,
I can't live on promises winter to spring.
Today is my moment and Now is my story,
I'll laugh and I'll cry and I'll sing. (And today . . .)

Knowing the importance of social commitment to
Jan and Ed, the singer added another verse for which
he had written a new tune:

And yet all around me, I hear children crying,
I feel the bombs falling, I see the suffering.
And so I'll keep working to make this world better,
To join with my brothers and sisters and sing.

Then the minister turned to Ed and asked:

Ed, will you have this woman to be your wedded
wife, to live together in the shared estate of matrimony?
Will you love her, comfort her, honor her and keep her,
in sickness and in health, in sorrow and in joy, according
to this bond of trust?
    I will.
    Jan, will you have this man to be your wedded

husband, to live together in the shared estate of matrimony? Will you love him, comfort him, honor and keep him, in sickness and in health, in sorrow and in joy, according to this bond of trust?

I will.

The minister then asked everyone to join in reading a poem by E. E. Cummings:

i thank You God for most this amazing
day:for the leaping greenly spirits of trees
and a blue true dream of sky;and for everything
which is natural which is infinite which is yes

(i who have died am alive again today,
and this is the sun's birthday;this is the birth
day of life and of love and wings:and of the gay
great happening illimitably earth)

how should tasting touching hearing seeing
breathing any—lifted from the no
of all nothing—human merely being
doubt unimaginable You?

(now the ears of my ears awake and
now the eyes of my eyes are opened)

The minister asked Jan and Ed to join right hands and turn toward one another. He asked Ed, then Jan, to repeat after him:

I, Ed, take you, Jan,
to be my wedded wife,
to love and to cherish,
for better, for worse,
for richer, for poorer,
in sickness and in health,
from this day forward.

I, Jan, take you, Ed
to be my wedded husband,
to love and to cherish,
for better, for worse,
for richer, for poorer,
in sickness and in health,
from this day forward.

The minister asked the couple, "What symbols do you offer in honor of this marriage?" They presented rings. "The circle of the ring is as love freely given: it has no beginning and it has no end." After saying a few words to her, Ed placed a ring on Jan's finger and said, "With this ring I marry you." After saying her own words to Ed, Jan placed a ring on his finger and said, "With this ring I marry you."

The minister poured a cup of wine and, holding it, said,

Into this cup is poured wine, bitter and sweet, even as life itself will pour into this marriage the varied bitterness and sweetness of life. Only in the deepest intimacy of man and woman may the bitterness of life be so blended with the sweet, that the love you share may be full and brave.

Many days you will sit at the same table and eat and drink together. Drink now, and may the cup of your life be rich and full to the running over.

After the bride and groom had drunk from the cup, the minister handed it to Ed who smashed it with his foot in keeping with the Jewish customs of his family.

Everyone then read aloud a portion of the poem "On Love" by Kahlil Gibran, and the minister said:

Let us be honest enough with ourselves to know that there is no true marriage, except the inward bond of trust and love that dwells in the hearts of Jan and Ed. Only they will know what marriage there is between them—the outer forms are only signs and covers over the love of their hearts.

We who are gathered here wish for them a good marriage. We pray that they may find together a richness beyond the wealth of money—a depth of soul that will make beautiful everything they do in life, separately, and together.

With joy in our hearts, we send them off with our deepest blessings.

Jan and Ed, having chosen one another from the many men and women of the earth, and having made their pledges to one another before this gathering, I hereby acknowledge that they are husband and wife.

Let all others honor them and the threshold of

their house. May they find here the good beginning for the spending of many years.

Finally, let us all join in the benediction, an Apache prayer:

> Now you will feel no rain, for each of you
> will be shelter to the other.
> Now you will feel no cold, for each of you
> will be warmth to the other.
> Now there is no loneliness for you;
> Now you are two persons, but there is only
> one life before you;
>
> Go now to your dwelling place, to enter into
> the days of your togetherness,
> And may your days be good, and long together.

The ceremony was over, and the guests and the wedding party crossed back over the bridge to the reception area. Everyone was silent for a time, reflecting on the ceremony. People gathered quietly around Jan and Ed, congratulating them and wishing them good luck.

Soon the steaks were sizzling on the fire. The feasting, singing, laughing, playing, hugging, and talking went on for several hours. At one point, everyone gathered to sing, but otherwise the guests were occupied with many activities. At dusk the reception ended and the guests went their many ways.

When it was all over, the wedding and reception had cost about four hundred dollars, a sum that covered food and drink for over eighty people, the park rental, and the minister's gift. Jan and Ed had looked for alternatives to the traditional wedding and reception—and they found, or made, a wedding that was truly personal.

It is to Jan and Ed that we owe the idea for this book.

2

The Emergence of
the Personal Wedding

THE PERSONAL WEDDING has revolutionized our society's way of thinking about the rites of marriage. Before the emergence of alternatives to the traditional ceremony, most couples never thought about what their wedding could be like if they wrote it themselves, chose the rituals they wanted, and involved themselves in the planning of their own service. But in the last decade, thousands of couples have reevaluated the old wedding traditions from a new perspective. Couples who desire more involvement, more personal interaction, more expression of themselves and the love they feel, have found the old ways lacking. Within a very short time, the couples who have chosen a more personal form of wedding have made the whole society aware that ancient customs could be used in a new way, and the wedding itself could be made a unique expression of commitment and festivity.

Journalists have been reporting on the shift away from traditional weddings for several years. In the July 4, 1969, issue of *Time* Magazine, one of their religion writers stated: "more and more couples are breaking away from traditional marriage ceremonies to invent their own." The article continued: "The stylized forms and archaic systems of the past appear increasingly irrelevant to some people, who, nonetheless, feel the need for some form of religious sanction for their love." Dr. B. Davie Napier, dean of the chapel at Stanford University admits, *Time* reported, "that he has become 'increasingly uneasy with a ceremony that doesn't speak to us now.'" Another change is that "many people no longer look to parents for assistance and advice" about weddings and marriage, so they rely heavily on friends for help. The idea of a parent "giving away" a daughter is no longer a fond one for many young women. The *Time* article ended with a thought that sums up what we found in our own research. "However far-out some of today's weddings tend to be, the need for ceremony remains deeply rooted. Pastors find this true even of couples who have been living together for some time before deciding on marriage. . . . while it takes new forms, they still want a sense of the mystical."

Business Week Magazine looked at another important aspect of weddings in its June 19, 1971, issue. In a marketing article titled "New Brides Ring Out the Old Traditions," the reporter recounts a sky-diving and a scuba-diving wedding, then says, "The trend is plain, and the multi-billion bridal industry is learning that tradition just does not count as much as it used to." More couples are getting married, but their dollar is going in new directions. "The patterns are definitely altering and perhaps the most important influence is sociological. Inflation and the wavering economy may give today's bride and groom pause in spending the way couples before them have spent, but that is a temporary restraint. Their outlook, however, points to deeper shifts. Some of today's couples, for example, will dispense with the wedding ceremony altogether—and that means no gowns, parties, catering, and gifts. Companies that depend on weddings 'with all the trimmings' are naturally worried."

And well they might be, as so many young couples today find the frills excessive and wasteful. The huge wedding, costing many thousands of dollars, is increasingly being viewed as "extravagant" to quote several people who responded to our questions. This idea of an expensive wedding is not being accepted by couples quite as readily today as it might have been ten or twenty years ago. And one of the primary reasons it is not popular is simply because there are good alternatives to this kind of grand affair and display. Couples are finding more new ways to celebrate their love. The direction is toward personal involvement and creation, not toward an empty bank book.

The *Business Week* article reports that catering services, expensive wedding gowns, and lavish honeymoons are on the slide. Since marriages are on the increase, this indicates that many thousands of couples are seeking alternatives.* Many brides are either mak-

* The National Center for Health Statistics reports 1,523,000 marriages in 1960, and 2,146,000 in 1969. *Life* magazine records 2,158,000 marriages in 1971. The *New York Times* reports 2,269,-000 for 1972—a jump of 111,000 weddings in one year. Divorce rates are also interesting: 377,000 in 1960, 733,000 in 1971, and 839,000 in 1972.

ing their own wedding gowns or getting married in clothes that have some possibility of being worn again. More honeymoons are tending to be camping trips, a time in the country, or a short trip abroad. The Grand Tour is virtually a thing of the past.

Financial bankruptcy is redeemable, but the spiritual bankruptcy described by Joan Didion in the *Saturday Evening Post* (December 16, 1967) is much more depressing. In her article, "Marrying Absurd," Ms. Didion describes the instant weddings of Las Vegas, Nevada. Anyone who has ever been there can remember the signs along the Strip advertising quickie wedding chapels. She says there are nineteen of these chapels competing for trade, most with neon signs selling "Sincerity," "Better Photos," "Candlelight with Your Ceremony," "Free Transportation," "Witnesses Available," and "Ample Parking." They are nothing but wedding mills, churning out instant couples. On the door of one chapel is a sign, not unlike those in television studios, warning another anxiously waiting couple, ONE MOMENT PLEASE—WEDDING.

Ms. Didion is disturbed by all this, especially the scene she described happening on August 26, 1965, the last day a man could hope to delay, through marriage, being drafted into the Army under President Johnson's revised draft board laws. On that day, 171 couples were married in or around Las Vegas. We understand the motives of the couples, but the weddings sound like an account from Dante's *Inferno*. Sixty-seven of the ceremonies were conducted by one justice of the peace that night. He told Ms. Didion of the scene, and his description sums up what many weddings may seem like to hundreds of Americans: " 'I got it [the ceremony] down from five minutes to three minutes,' he said. 'I could've married them *en masse,* but they're people, not cattle. People expect more when they get married.' "

People *do* expect more. Personal ceremonies attempt to affirm new values and new hopes in marriage. By choosing to plan their own ceremonies, using rituals or customs from a variety of religions and cultures, couples have added new vitality and spirit to one of mankind's most ancient rites. In effect, the entire premise of the ceremony itself—that everyone gets married by the same rituals in order to perpetuate a cohesive social or religious bond—has been turned around. Personal weddings assert an individuality and independence that runs counter to the traditional ideas of the ceremony. The old way of marrying simply did not meet enough of the needs people felt. The rigidity of Protestant, Catholic, and Jewish services did not allow for varying expressions of joy, or the participation of guests, or the inclusion of poems, songs, or dance. By rejecting traditional forms many couples found they could become more personally involved in all parts of the wedding—rituals, vows, prayers, readings, and music.

This desire for more personal weddings may not be surprising, but why did the change happen when it did? Weddings are social events, and they often indicate the moods and the movements of a society. To get some idea of why the personal wedding emerged when it did, we have to take a broad look at the social forces that were emerging in the 1960s.

The changes in society produced by the civil rights movement and the opposition to the war in Vietnam are obvious now. Social activism and demands for new political priorities were widespread, involving national issues as well as personal decisions about how to live one's life with integrity and happiness. Some observers have stated that the young people who were most active in deploring racial discrimination and war were the same ones who eventually began looking for alternative wedding styles.

But it was the sudden changes in three other areas —the churches, the life-styles of people, and the role of women both in the home and outside it—that contributed most directly to the alterations in wedding traditions. Many churches began to relax their old customs of matrimony. Hundreds of thousands of young people sought more human and honest ways of living and communicating, which for women included equality with men in society at large as well as in the structure of marriage. Along with these changes came a more modern and realistic view of the wedding itself. The marriage ceremony began to take on new form and new substance.

The Second Vatican Council and the influence of Pope John XXIII helped millions of Catholics and Protestants think about their religion in new ways. Catholicism changed many of its customs, translated its liturgy into the vernacular, and generally loosened its control over old traditions. Protestant religions also altered many of their customs; a different tone began to be heard and felt in churches. Some members of the clergy and their congregations began to value new forms of celebration in services and rites. Lay people started playing a far more significant role in services. Churches experimented with different ways of honoring God and humanity, and most people seemed to find a new sense of joy and worship in their religions.

When people began questioning the value of traditional wedding ceremonies, many churches were ready and willing to entertain alternatives. Couples who were trying to express their care and love for each other in their weddings found a new sense of acceptance of the personal wedding, especially among younger priests, ministers, and rabbis. On July 1, 1969, the Catholic church substantially widened the elective elements of the liturgy for weddings. The Lutheran and Episcopal churches have been revising their traditional services by updating the language, offering more chances for participation by guests, and giving more choices to the couple for what can be said and done in the ceremony. Most other denominations are implementing or considering similar changes. Within a remarkably short time, personal weddings, which had begun largely as unconventional reactions against the rigidities of church traditions, have been accepted and even encouraged throughout the land.

The emphasis on different life-styles in the last decade is familiar to everyone. The most publicized of hundreds of variations have been the new clothing style, the communes, encounter groups, experimentation with drugs, and the popularity of Eastern religions. But there have been other, less sensational, life-styles, too. Conformity to social norms has meant little to millions of young Americans who are searching for personal guidelines and answers to the questions that confront them. Every aspect of traditional living has been closely scrutinized, and for many, the Madison Avenue idea of a fulfilling life has been found wanting.

The movement from acceptance to questioning and altering shows itself clearly in wedding ceremonies. The old rituals simply did not speak to couples who wanted to promote and publicize their view of life and marriage. Personal qualities had taken on more importance than institutional ones, and the emphasis in weddings began to change accordingly. The life-style of a couple no longer had to be masked in a white dress and black tuxedo, or in words that had little real meaning to the couple.

The changes within the churches and the greater freedom of individual life-styles had their effect, but the most significant change affecting weddings and the institution of marriage itself has been the growth of a women's movement determined to equalize the roles of men and women in the home and in society. Other movements in the 1960s actively promoted equality for all people, rich or poor, black or white. Yet the unequal position of women had not been confronted directly since the suffrage movement culminated in the ratification of the Nineteenth Amendment in 1920. When, in the late 1960s, the renewed Women's Liberation Movement actively took up the issues of the discrepancies between the treatment of men and women in society, most people took notice. In many cases the inequities were too obvious to dismiss. How are women going to be treated in the employment field? Do they have the same rights as men? What about child care? And within the family structure, can the traditional roles be made more equal? These questions were—and are—being asked by more and more people. For many women contemplating marriage, they are central.

A new awareness about the relationship between men and women has changed a large part of the younger generation's thinking about the roles assumed to be proper for each sex. Many are trying to work out relationships that are more open, freer for experimentation. There is a conscious attempt to allow each partner the opportunity to pursue his or her own interests, growth, and relationships without the ancient stigma of the double standard. Personal weddings, which usually stress a new and more equal role relationship between husband and wife, really could not have emerged if women were not free to share in all aspects of married life. A large number of couples who have moved away from traditional wedding services have done so because they wanted to express their feelings and intentions about their equality in marriage in new and more precise ways. By personalizing their ceremonies, they are more able to reflect these changed priorities and values; more able to represent what they see as their new position in society in more honest terms.

All of these changes—social and personal—in weddings and marriage have been swift and, in some cases, dramatic. Some people have been confused by the rejection of traditions and have asked why so many couples believe that the old tried and true ways are not good enough. We see two answers to these questions.

First, weddings and marriage styles ought to reflect the values of both individuals involved. How a couple choose to conduct their wedding is often indicative of how much thought and spirit they are willing to put into their life together. The growing number of people who are rejecting "tradition for its own sake" and are searching for their own ways to express their personalities and experiences are affecting change on the entire society, too. They are looking for ways to live in this last third of the century—and into the next —so their lives, and their children's, will have validity and meaning now. In rejecting prescribed formulas for propriety and social acceptance, these people are encouraging others to question their own values and needs. Second, wedding traditions and practices are a social barometer recording the mood of a culture or a country. Uncritical compliance with strict wedding traditions usually indicates the same general compliance with most other social or political norms and laws. When the American ethic was primarily one of hard work, fitting in, and monetary success, weddings were almost always traditional within each culture's bounds. Each new wave of immigrants brought its own wedding rituals, which were usually one of the last aspects of that ethnic heritage to change as the second and third generation became more Americanized. But in most cases now, except for recent immigrants, the old-country styles have changed drastically. Some old rituals are kept, but a large number of young people today are going far beyond the accepted traditions of their ancestors, forming new styles that are more suited for themselves. Thus this social barometer—a group's wedding rituals—indicates not a surface fad, but a very deep change in that group's views and values.

Life's three most honored and spiritual events are birth, marriage, and death. How a group of people celebrate or mourn these events tells an observer a great deal about their society. A segment of any group that diverges from the norm to search out new directions has, historically, often produced reevaluation and change. That is happening now. In the case of weddings, the people who have decided against the accepted nuptial celebration have largely been seeking new ways to express themselves, their relation to the world, and their love for one another.

We see a clear correlation between the phenomena discussed above—receptivity to change within the churches, increasing diversity in all aspects of life-style, and growing equality in male-female relationships and roles—and the emergence of the personal wedding. All these areas indicate a profound shift in social rules and norms. The shift is toward more freedom of expression, toward growth in the individual, and, one may hope, toward more joy in life.

In researching the emergence and growth of personal weddings, we talked to hundreds of people, through personal interviews and written questions, to learn from their experiences. One question we asked was "How did you first hear about personal weddings and what was your reaction to them?" A man from Wisconsin said: "The first I heard about personal weddings was those kids in California, back in the sixties. I thought it was pretty strange at the time. But, then, I also liked the idea. They all seemed to be having a good time, and in my family, everyone gets worried and short tempered for a good month before a wedding. In a way, I thought those kids had the right idea. Getting married should be fun."

Not everyone agreed, of course. Some people were

outraged—a travesty, they claimed. Others were puzzled. A woman from Pennsylvania wrote us: "I couldn't (and can't today) understand being so casual about a wedding. You can have a picnic in the park any weekend you want and invite all your friends. But you only get married once . . . or these days, maybe twice! So why not make it something special, something people will remember and you will remember."

"What the early personal weddings did for us," a woman from Texas replied, "was to help us think about different things we could do in our own wedding. For one thing, I never liked the idea of my father 'giving me away' like I was a piece of merchandise or a prize farm animal. I also didn't like the part in the service where it says 'to love, honor and obey.' Love and honor, yes. But obey—forget it! I may be getting picky, but I also didn't like that bit, 'I now pronounce you man and wife.' To me that's like saying he's a person and I'm his possession. It's just as ridiculous as saying, 'I now pronounce you woman and husband.' So Jerry and I talked it over and agreed to make a few changes in our service. Nothing dramatic, you know, but enough to make us feel more honest about the whole thing."

The famous saying, "There is nothing more powerful than an idea whose time has come" certainly seems to apply here. Before, individuals had seldom questioned the immutability of traditional weddings, but they put up with them because there were no real alternatives. Now people are questioning the customs traditional to their own religion, culture, or social class, and are beginning to move beyond them. They are modifying the old rituals and creating new ones.

The people we interviewed had many diverse opinions about what a marriage ceremony should be like—for themselves. Most of them had formed definite ideas about their own weddings; ideas that set their own wedding apart from everyone else's. We asked most of the people we spoke with about their reasons for going beyond a traditional wedding ceremony.

A woman from New York: "For me, a wedding should be a beginning. It's a symbol of what your life is going to be like together. When Gary and I got engaged, we wondered what we would really be saying if we had a traditional wedding. What would it mean? That our life is going to be like everybody else's life? That Gary will go to work and I'll just have kids and stay at home and raise them? And we'll have a house in the suburbs and live happily ever after? That isn't what either of us wanted for ourselves. My older sister did it that way, and now she's getting a divorce after six years. I stopped believing in that dream a long time ago. Neither Gary nor I wanted a wedding that implied those values, either. We made our wedding different from the usual because we wanted it to symbolize a life that would be different—one with more interaction, acceptance, and caring—more flexible roles. We wrote most of our own ceremony with the help of a minister friend who suggested different passages from the Bible. Another friend chose and played the music. We really created our own little world there. And I think it was beautiful. We wanted to achieve a very special feeling for ourselves and our guests, and we did."

A man from California: "Susan and I had been living together for two years before we decided to get married. A lot of our friends were living the same way. We decided we wanted kids, and we're middle-class enough that we wanted to have our relationship legal. But when it came down to planning the ceremony it got really absurd. What were we going to do? Have the bride wear white and have some minister say it was O.K. for me to kiss her now, and then have people wish us phony congratulations on our new life together? What a scene! It would have been such a farce, especially since all our friends and relatives knew the score. So we got a lot of quotes together from books we loved—and from songs—and put together our own service. Not too religious, either. Susan and I tried to say to each other what this new commitment meant to us. We both felt that the decision to have kids had changed us and brought us even closer. We wanted to celebrate that. We invited the same people we would have invited if we'd done it the straight way, but the ceremony was fun. People seemed to enjoy the difference. Even my folks liked it—probably because we had done it ourselves. The ceremony took some time to put together since we had to hunt up all those quotes, but that was fun, too. And you know, one of the nicest things was that an old lady, one of Susan's aunts, said to us she thought it was the 'most honest' wedding she'd ever seen. I really think she meant it."

A woman from Virginia: "When Peter and I got married we broke a lot of old rules, but we made up for it by adding things that meant much more to us. I've been involved in the Women's Liberation Movement for a couple of years now—and growing angrier all the time at the position of women in this country of ours. One of the things Peter and I did for each other was to spell out beforehand how we wanted to structure our married life—what responsibilities were mine, what were his. Who would work when and how much money would we need. That kind of thing. We made a loose contract of sorts. I wanted this not so much because I thought Peter would turn on me and shackle me down once we were married, but because I wanted my ideals and values made public, at the wedding. I didn't want anyone to be mistaken and think we were just another young couple doing the usual thing. (I'm afraid this sounds too much like only I had these ideals. Peter agrees completely. He was the one who suggested the contract in the first place.) So our wedding vows were actually what we agreed to in the contract, which essentially declared our own separate identities and our equality as two people in a journey together in matrimony. Neither of us could bear a sort of master-slave relationship. I have interests that don't agree with Peter's. But we don't feel that either of us has to capitulate to the other just because we're married.

"The main thing is that we made these feelings public. It's hard to explain what a difference this has made in my own growth, or Peter's, but it's been huge. I think we've avoided a lot of the hassles I see my friends going through who are fighting about who does what, who gets to go where, etc. I think we got away from some of the deviousness that can easily happen in a marriage by trying to get as much as possible out in the open. To me, that's a lot of what love is. We've revised our contract several times in the two and a half years we've been married, but the structure still stands firm."

A man from Illinois: "I've been married twice. For my first wedding, we went through the whole ordeal—tux, white dress, lots of flowers, about twelve attendants, and a very expensive caterer. I don't recall what the bill came to, but it seemed extraordinary—over three thousand dollars. I remember how both of our families got so upset about how many guests from each family could come, who would sit where, and so forth. Our mothers were arguing politely, and we felt like a couple of kids. When the ceremony finally came, I felt stiff and unnatural. The starched collar was itching my neck. I felt like I'd been stuffed into the outfit. I was very nervous—scared I'd trip or do something stupid. I just wished the whole thing would be over so I could get out of my costume and away from all the hassles. It was a terrible feeling. That whole myth about the wedding day being so great, and all I wanted to do was get out of those clothes and away with my new wife. It's funny now, I suppose, but it wasn't then. The whole buildup beforehand is so much trouble. I felt like my wedding was just a hurdle that had to be gotten over, something to be done with so the real living could begin. Really a bad way to begin, isn't it?

"But the second time I got married I said NO MORE of that. My second wife had been married once before, too, so she totally agreed. Who can go through a thing like that twice? We had a small, simple ceremony. We didn't want to write our own vows or that kind of thing, but we also didn't want to be married with the exact same words as had been used the first time, with other partners. The minister changed a few things around. He chose different things from the Bible and read those. He talked with us, not to us, and it was very different. I wasn't nervous. I didn't have the feeling that something might go wrong. It was just very natural. I enjoyed it so much more because I felt more a part of it. And I could breathe, too!"

A woman from Massachusetts: "My husband and I were married on Cape Cod, on a beach in Truro at sunset. We thought that was a place where we would feel the most peaceful because we loved it so much. The guests wore casual dress; a few just came in swim suits, and several people who happened to be on the beach joined us, too. Neither of us belonged to any church, so a justice of the peace was our officiant. Everything went wonderfully. Everyone chanted and sang and joined in our happiness. It was glorious and beautiful to be there outside in the wind. I'll never lose the feeling of that night."

A woman from Ohio: "I couldn't see spending thousands of dollars on a wedding. My parents were all ready to rent the biggest, fanciest ballroom, get an expensive caterer and band and all the trimmings. I tried not to hurt their feelings, but one day I just said, 'Look, I know what you want but it's not what I want.' I couldn't see any reason not to have the wedding at our house—it's big enough for the number of guests we invited. Neither of us was trying to impress anyone, especially with a lot of gaudy stuff.

"The other thing, you know, is that Dave and I wanted to be a part of everything—not have it all done for us. I didn't want to feel like I was being waited on. I guess that's because my father has a lot of money and

I grew up with material things that aren't important to me anymore. I'm trying to get away from all that now, and so is Dave. And the money involved! My 'social guilt' or whatever you call it just wouldn't let us waste money that way.

"Our wedding was celebrated in our backyard garden on a lovely summer day. It couldn't have been more perfect. Dave has a group of friends who play classical music with flutes and violins. They came and played most of the time. Everyone dressed casually and roamed around freely. Our ceremony was fairly standard for our religion, and we added our own touches by reading three poems (two by E. E. Cummings and one by James Joyce). The reception was also in the yard. It was so much easier that way. People stayed for hours and sang with the musicians and danced to records later. Dave and I were having so much fun we didn't want to leave for our honeymoon! It was just the kind of wedding we wanted. My parents were pleased, too. I could tell they felt proud of us."

A man from New York: "The standard litany of my church's wedding service was full of vows I couldn't accept. Like the line, 'till death us do part.' It's a fine sentiment, but not all that realistic today, is it? I want to try to make our marriage last our lifetime, but not if it turns out to be a prison. My own life means more than having to endure a bad marriage just so things look good to the neighbors. Besides, everyone knows that something like one out of every three marriages ends in divorce anyway. That line didn't ring true for me.

"A lot of friends of ours, married a few years, are finding that they want very different things from their lives, so they're splitting up, and it's very unhappy. They all had this 'till death us do part' business drummed into them, so there's lots of guilt being spread around—when maybe there shouldn't be. They want different things to stay alive spiritually, and each one should have that option, especially when maybe another person can help them attain it.

"When Jane and I got married—and I must say we waited quite a while before we decided to get married—we changed that line to 'as long as we both shall love' and felt a lot more honest about it. If one of us wants out in the future, maybe it will be easier or less vindictive if we don't feel stuck with those old vows. The good thing about the changes we made in our ceremony is that we tried to face up to some things early on—I mean, that it may not last a lifetime, that it wasn't going to be all rosy. We've been together for five years now, and we're going strong. We're both in this marriage for 'love,' and I hope it will last for life."

A man from Minnesota: "My ideas for my wedding are a result of sitting through so many similar ceremonies—I mean ones that were identical. I hated that. So I decided a long time ago to vary my own ceremony. I went to a lot of weddings during my college years, but after a while, I skipped the wedding and showed up at the reception. What had I missed? All my friends got married with the exact same ceremony and words. The receptions were good; everybody relaxed and drank and danced. But the weddings. Nothing doing. All you have to do is sit through a few traditional ceremonies and you know how unspecial a wedding can be for the guests."

A woman from Washington: "I feel uncomfortable when I'm 'performing,' and that's how I knew I'd feel (Jim, too) as long as we stood at the altar and our friends and relatives sat behind us. Maybe it was partly stagefright, but I didn't want the usual set-up. With our priest's help, Jim and I decided to involve everyone in the ceremony. In physical arrangements and in participation. We all stood in a large circle. The priest asked people to speak or read something for or to us. (We told our guests ahead of time, of course, but even so, a few were surprised and even a little uncomfortable at first.) I was so nervous about getting married that I wasn't totally aware of how they felt, but I sensed most of our friends relaxed pretty fast and were really participating in the ceremony. The comments we heard afterward were very positive. In fact, one of Jim's relatives said he felt as if he had gotten married all over again! One of my friends said she felt so close in spirit to everyone during the ceremony that she almost believed the whole group was getting married. I loved that. It made me feel that Jim and I brought something entirely new into our marriage."

The opinions and experiences of all these people are personal and subjective. Each one was looking for a way to have his or her wedding speak for the couple, become part of the couple, in word and deed. No one that we spoke with had begun with a complete "master plan" in mind. But in talking over ideas, the couples evolved their own ceremony. No one had a single formula to follow. And most people said half the fun of their ceremony was creating it for themselves by digging through books, talking with others, and writing their own material. That is a big part of what it is to have a personal wedding. Nevertheless, there are basic elements of similarity or agreement that one can discern running through these very personal ceremonies and celebrations.

The following six points are not gospel (although we think the news is good), but they do summarize the elements that seem to be most important to couples who have created their own personal weddings.

Celebration

A wedding is a time of joy and celebration, reflecting the love and respect, excitement and honor, that the participants feel for each other. These feelings can be shown in dozens of ways. Music, decorations, flowers, dancing, feasting, poetry, and prayer—all can contribute to the tone of the celebration. What is said and what is done, by the couple and the co-celebrants, sets the tone and mood.

Expression of Uniqueness

A wedding also reflects the couple's values, interests, and tastes. Few occasions are more personal than one's wedding. Each element can be made an expression of personal values and interests. Where will the wedding take place? What do we say to each other? What kind of music do we want? What type of reception shall we have? Couples who decide these questions for themselves are reflecting their personal concern for all aspects of the wedding celebration.

Symbolic Beginning

The couples we interviewed worked out their own wedding rituals *not* just to be different, but to symbolize the kind of life they hoped to lead together. Even couples who had lived together before their marriage said that the wedding symbolized a further degree of commitment for them. One couple planning to devote much of their time to the preservation of the wilderness held their wedding in a forest clearing and served only natural foods and wine at their rustic reception. Another couple, wanting to reflect the equality they intended in their role relationships, read their contract to their guests and also shared in the serving of food and drink at the reception. Their weddings were not "obstacles and hassles to be gotten over," but very real attempts to begin their married lives with the commitments they honored in mind.

If in planning one partner seems to make all the decisions, it is likely that the same decision-making process will carry over into the marriage—how the couple furnish their home, raise their children, entertain their guests, and so on. For this reason, many couples we talked to emphasized how important it was to them that they plan their wedding *together* and work through their differences in a productive way, not a way where one is the winner and one is the loser. For this was how they hoped to live together. Similarly, the amount of money couples spend on their wedding and what they choose to spend it on is often symbolic of how they will manage money throughout their lives. One couple used the money that might have been spent on an expensive wedding to make a down payment on a piece of property in the mountains. Another chose to use a good deal of money to fly in friends from different parts of the country who could not otherwise have attended. A third couple chose to limit their expenses to one hundred dollars because they did not plan on "wasting" money in their married life. A fourth spent quite a lot on their wedding. They both enjoyed having lavish parties and planned on doing a lot more of that after they were married. In each case, the choice about wedding expenditures set the tone for similar financial choices in the marriage. It was a symbolic beginning for the couple being married.

Honesty

Many personal weddings have striven for authenticity and a genuine spirit—free from role-playing and free from unrealistic promises and expectations. Sometimes this is accomplished through the choice of the site for the ceremony or reception, or through the unpretentious spirit that surrounds the whole occasion. This honesty to self, and the couple's dual self, can be readily seen when a couple follows the dictates of their own minds, not social conventions.

Participation

People who have personal weddings often try to involve their friends and relatives in the service. We've heard various reasons, but the main one is that the couples value full participation. They don't want an audience, a word whose root means "to hear." They want co-celebrants. In some weddings, people have brought poems to read for the couple; in others, the co-celebrants have simply stated their feelings at the moment or just said something as simple as, "Good luck, we love you." Participation has been valuable at the receptions, too. At one wedding, friends were asked to bring a musical instrument; a whole band was formed and played for hours. At another, guests were asked to help celebrate by bringing a favorite food. Most of them out-did themselves and prepared exotic dishes. The aim of these couples has been to have their close friends and relatives genuinely share their joy.

Respect

Respect takes many forms, and in the personal weddings we've seen and heard of, it was demonstrated in many ways. The couples have wanted their weddings to show that they respected themselves. While dress has often been casual, it has not been sloppy. Couples have demonstrated in their general bearing and demeanor and in their words that they hold each other in high esteem.

Second, couples who have planned personal weddings have shown respect for their relatives and friends. Even though many couples formed new rituals, they were not "flying in the face of tradition" for the sake of rebellion or showing off. Their rituals were deeply thought out, and ones that added to their appreciation for the mystical and the real. They did not want their friends, and especially their relatives, to be uncomfortable. Although these couples departed from the traditional, they did it in a tasteful way that took into consideration their families' feelings and expectations.

Finally, respect for God and religious beliefs has

been evident in most of these personal wedding ceremonies. A minister has usually been present, although the minister's role has sometimes changed. Biblical passages have been read and prayers offered, although not always the traditional ones. And for those couples who did not believe in God or an organized religion, respect has usually been shown to nature, spiritualism, or some other higher order.

These six elements seem to encompass much of the spirit and care in personal weddings. They are not offered as criteria for having a personal ceremony, but merely as the direction in which many couples have moved when rethinking and changing the traditional ceremony. It is impossible to define exactly what a personal wedding is or should be. That decision is one each couple must make for themselves. But in talking with a large number of people—black and white, Christian and Jew, rural and urban—we found a basic similarity in focus and intent. Each couple wanted a ceremony that was part of them in all ways, that used new or modified rituals, and that met their expanding human awareness and needs. They weren't interested in the form of the wedding as much as they were in what the ceremony meant to them and their guests.

These six values allow for an enormous diversity in weddings. Both in appearance and substance, a couple is now freer than ever before to vary elements and have a wedding that expresses their relationship to each other and their new place in society. This is the real meaning and value of the personal wedding today.

THE HANDBOOK
FOR
PERSONAL
WEDDINGS

3

The Handbook for Personal Weddings

THIS SECTION IS DESIGNED as a handbook, in which any particular phase of wedding planning can be easily referred to and considered. Very simply, we want this part of the book to be of practical use to couples, families, friends, officiants, and congregations who are personally involved in designing, conducting, and participating in a wedding. For those readers who are not presently involved in an actual wedding, this section will provide much more detailed documentation for the historical changes in traditional wedding and marriage practices discussed in other chapters.

In this handbook we are trying to help in the decision-making process in two ways: (1) by calling attention to the major issues you will have to face in planning a personal wedding, and (2) by offering several suggestions or raising questions about each issue so as to expand your view of what is possible as you seek alternatives that have special meaning for you.

Our purpose is not to establish a whole new set of "traditional-alternative weddings," although, ironically, any listing of specific choices that run counter to an established norm tends to take on an air of orthodoxy in itself. Rather, our purpose is to set down a portion of the great variety of ways that people have recently "gone to the altar" in order to suggest some of the possible options you have before you. We hope it will be used simply as a handbook—a guide to stimulate your thinking and a reference to help you remember the issues you want to consider.

The ideas in this section have come from individuals or couples from all over the country, of all ages, religions, and races. Each couple had to contend with certain norms, expectations, desires, and sometimes pressures from their families, friends, and religious faiths. But more importantly, there was also a desire in each couple to have their wedding reflect their own uniqueness, their own values, and their own reality. Their alternatives need not be yours.

Borrow freely if you like. Change and adapt the ideas you find here. Create entirely new alternatives. In the final analysis, whether or not you have a personal wedding depends not on its outward form, but whether you have chosen each part of the wedding according to your own values and your own goals. One way or another, you give yourselves in marriage.

ENGAGEMENT

Most couples become engaged, formally or informally, before they seriously discuss wedding plans. Whether a ring is given or not, the engagement marks the beginning of long talks about "what our wedding will be like." But we've heard of several alternatives to the traditional engagement period, ring giving, announcements, and parties.

While still acknowledging the engagement, a majority of the people we questioned did not place as much value on this period as generations in the past have done. There is a far more laissez-faire attitude about formal engagements nowadays. The engagement ring is a token of promise, yet one that thousands feel they can forgo since the emotional promise is far more valuable than the symbol. Another reason is that, with many couples living together before marriage, the old-style, formal engagement is not needed. Their living together is a new form of engagement.

When a couple decides to get married, the two most common ways of letting the world know about it are (1) announcements in the newspaper and (2) a party.

If you want to announce your marriage in your local newspaper, call the society editor and find out exact requirements about photographs, length of your announcement, costs, if any, and so on. If you are from different towns or cities, it is customary to send the announcement to both newspapers. If you don't care for this type of advertisement, you can send out letters to close friends and relatives, or call them, or go visit them yourselves. We have heard of people buying radio time to make their announcement or even hiring a sky-writer plane; but these practices tend to get expensive. Other couples don't make any formal announcement at all. They simply mention their plans, in random fashion, to whichever friends and relatives they happen to see, and trust the grapevine to inform everyone else.

Many couples also celebrate their engagement with a party—often making the announcement of their engagement right at the party, surprising all the guests. You can give the party yourselves, or a close friend or relative can give it for you. All these approaches are typical. It tends to be a time for lots of handshaking, hugging, and congratulations. Any type of formal engagement announcement or party is also likely to elicit presents from many relatives and friends. Whether or not you wish to encourage such gifts is a factor you might want to consider as you decide how you will announce your engagement.

However, the main focus here is not really the engagement, but the wedding. So let us assume that you have announced your engagement and celebrated the occasion in whatever way was most comfortable for you. At some point, attention shifts from the present to the future as you begin to think ahead toward your wedding. For some couples, this may come right after their engagement. Others may plan on delaying their marriage for several months. But in any case, assuming the engagement period has no unpleasant surprises, there comes a time when each couple decides to get married. And that's when the planning really begins.

PRE-WEDDING PLANNING

Pre-wedding planning adds up to about 90 percent of the work involved in having a successful, beautiful wedding. The decisions you make in the beginning about the size, style, site, and season of your ceremony are going to influence dozens of other planning decisions you will be making as the wedding draws nearer. So it is natural that right from the start couples begin asking themselves some very specific questions like these:

When will it be? Where do we want the ceremony to take place? How much can we afford to spend? Whom should we invite? Who will officiate? What shall we wear?

But these questions, although they may be the first to occur to a couple, are not the most basic questions of all. Underlying each of them is another series of questions—ones that are often overlooked. And so a couple may find that, although they planned their guest list carefully, they feel very separate from their friends and relatives as they stand there at the altar. Or they may discover that the clothes they had selected so meticulously feel uncomfortable and unnatural on their wedding day. Or the money that they calculated accurately they could afford to spend seemed, in the end, not to have been worth it.

Unfortunately, these couples did not recognize beforehand that many of the decisions in planning a wedding are not ends in themselves, but are only means toward other ends. And the real ends or goals of a wedding must be discovered by a very different series of questions:

What does this day mean to us?

What do we want our wedding to accomplish?

What atmosphere do we want to achieve—intimate, impressive, wealthy, celebrative, worshipful, gay?

Do we value privacy and intimacy more than a large number of family and friends?

Do we think of our ceremony as a short worship service or a time for lengthy community sharing?

What are our feelings about the importance of ritual?

Is our love best unspoken or only briefly expressed, or is the nature of our commitment such that we want to publically affirm, in detail, the terms of our marriage contract and vows?

Basically these are questions of *values*. If you choose to have a totally traditional wedding, then the value questions are, for the most part, answered for you by the customs of your religion, state, parents, social group, and so on. But if you start from a different premise—that there is hardly anything in your wedding that need be taken for granted, that almost every facet of the event is up to you, then you are definitely forced into a fairly deep consideration of your values —as individuals and as partners.

Not that these questions of values are ever answered all at once. It seems that couples who plan their own weddings tend to go back and forth between the deeper values questions and the nuts-and-bolts decisions that stem from them. As they accept and reject specific alternatives for decorations, or food, or guests, they become gradually clearer about what effect they are trying to achieve in their wedding. Similarly, as a major value becomes clearer, all the more mundane decisions that follow from it are vastly simplified.

Again and again, *finances* will come up as an issue needing consideration. Money seems to play a part in

many of our basic decisions in life, and it is no different with a wedding. Specific financial questions will be
covered in many of the following sections, but here we
want to raise the issue of the values you follow in regard to your wedding spending.

First, it is a totally personal matter. We know
that marriages can be accomplished for as little as the
cost of a marriage license, and we know also that some
parents have spent as much as $50,000 on their chil-
dren's weddings. To some of us, $50,000 for a wedding
would appear obscene. But for many people in the
world, even a modest wedding which costs, for example, only $400, would seem just as extravagant. Which
of us is so wise as to know, for others, the "right
amount" to spend on a wedding?

Nevertheless, among couples planning their own
weddings, the definite trend seems to be toward for-
going ornate, lavish weddings—even when the couple's
parents can afford them—and instead, concentrating
on having simple, tasteful affairs they plan themselves.
In most of the sections that follow, alternatives are
offered for reducing the cost of the wedding while
maintaining most of the other values. There is no one
section devoted to finances, so we call special attention
to it here, as an issue which is all-pervasive in planning
a wedding. It will undoubtedly be a values issue that
you will want to discuss right at the beginning and to
keep on discussing whenever it comes up with respect
to a particular decision you have to make.

After talking over the numerous aspects of
finances and other major decisions involving values, it
won't be long before you come back again to some

important, specific questions which need answers. As always, how you determine your solutions to these problems will show on your wedding day. What you put in now, by choices, planning, and creativity, will be very apparent later on.

PRACTICAL PLANNING

After you have a general idea of what kind and style of wedding you want, you're ready to deal with these six major decisions:

1. When will we have our wedding?
2. Where will it be?
3. What time of day or night?
4. Whom shall we invite?
5. Who will officiate?
6. Where will the reception be held?

CHOICE OF DATE: Like all the other decisions above, when to have the wedding is strictly personal. How long do you have to or want to wait before getting married? What season or month do you like best? What are the advantages and disadvantages of each date you are considering? Obviously, if you're planning an outdoor celebration the warmer months are best suited.

In choosing a date, a major question to ask is: have we given ourselves enough time to prepare for the kind of wedding we want? Remember that in most cases you'll either have to rent a place for a reception or make some other arrangements that may take time.

Also, if you want a church wedding, give yourselves ample time to choose the date you want. Clergymen are often booked up weeks or months in advance. *You* may be ready to get married, but the minister may not have time. Some weddings can be put together in a matter of a few weeks and go smoothly. Others require much more time. If you want to be married on a beach, with the reception at a friend's home, then your time crunch won't be as bad as if you want St. Patrick's Cathedral and the Plaza Hotel. Just be sure you can do all the things that are called for, while avoiding the enormous strain and pressure that can come from not having enough time for the planning.

In choosing the actual day of your wedding, try to leave time for those who work a five- or six-day week or who must travel to get to the site. Saturday is the most popular day for Christians, but it is against Jewish law to wed on Friday night or Saturday. The more you sense that your guests are comfortable and relaxed on your wedding day, the more you will enjoy your wedding; so choose the day with them in mind, too.

LOCATION: Where to hold the ceremony is another important question in any wedding. We encourage you to find a location that has some special meaning to you, wherever it may be—your house, a certain church (if the pastor is willing), an outdoor site. Some couples have even traveled to foreign countries to be married in their own special place.

One large factor to keep in mind in choosing a location is the cost. Some places will cost nothing or very little; others, like hotels or other commercial establishments, will be more. If money is a consideration, this is one area in which you can save considerably. Communities often require a municipal permit for use of a public place, like a park or beach, if more than a dozen or so people are expected to assemble. Information about such regulations can usually be obtained from the local police or other town officials.

Many of the alternative weddings we know of did not take place in a church. The list of possible places seems almost endless. Here are a few examples:

1. On a beach at sunrise.
2. On the shore of a lake.
3. In a secluded part of a city or town park.
4. In the new home of the bride and groom.
5. On top of a mountain.
6. In a bird sanctuary.
7. In a friend's—or your own—backyard.

We could fill a dozen more pages with examples, but that isn't the point. What you want to decide on is a location that is personally satisfying, accessible, legal, and, whether indoors or out, beautiful. No matter where you live, you have the option between indoor and outdoor weddings, and in many cases nature offers the choicest settings. Just remember these points: if you choose an indoor location, is it large enough to accommodate the number of people you want to invite; and, if it is outdoors, have you made some kind of arrangement for an indoor or sheltered retreat in case of bad weather? If you've planned for disasters as well as the good moments, you'll probably find the weeks before the wedding a whole lot more relaxing. You'll know that even a rainy day can't spoil everything.

TIME OF DAY OR NIGHT: Most cultures and religions have acquired traditional times for weddings to take place. Clearly, once a couple realizes that their wedding is *theirs* to plan, then any hour of the day or night becomes a possibility.

Most weddings, even personal weddings, still take place sometime during the middle of the day. A smaller, though significant, number also take place during the evening. However we have noted an increase in the number of weddings taking place at three other times—at sunrise, at sunset, and at midnight. It is interesting to consider how each of these times of day or night has definite spiritual or mystical qualities for most people. The sense of wonder, the sense of awe, the sense of the unknown possibilities of life seem present at each of the three times. While the general trend in personal weddings is away from the primitive-based rituals and in favor of more modern and consciously meaningful rituals, in this one area the trend seems reversed.

At each of these times—sunrise, sunset, and midnight—feasting seems a natural follow-up, whether in the form of breakfast, dinner, or a midnight feast.

Perhaps you prefer a midday or evening wedding. But given the season and location you've chosen, it is possible that another time of day or night might greatly enhance the effect you want to achieve.

It is traditional, even in the above examples, to regard the time for a wedding as being that time devoted to the service and the reception which usually follows the service. It is worth noting that more and more couples are extending the duration of their "wedding" by inviting guests for whole days or even entire weekends. In so doing, they build a whole series of activities, ceremonies, and meals into this time period, creating not only a more memorable occasion, but a sense of community among the two families and all the friends.

GUESTS: The number of guests you'll have at the wedding and reception will depend on several other decisions: (1) the type of ceremony you want to have, (2) how many people the place of both the wedding and the reception can accommodate comfortably, (3) what style of reception you are planning, and (4) how much money you can afford to spend.

These are all big issues—but, then, so is an enormous bill after the reception is over. Limiting guests is difficult, but if you are limited by funds or space or the style you want, you'll end up having to cut your list down to realistic terms. If you are planning an outdoor wedding and reception, and money is no problem, then you and your parents can draw up a nice long list, if you like. Or, if you can solve the reception problem by lowering costs, then again, you can invite more guests.

But what if space and money are serious considerations? What then? Here there are many alternatives, too. Space problems can usually be solved by people standing instead of sitting, by moving furniture or in other ways redesigning a room. However, space usually isn't the major concern—money is. If your food and drink budget comes out to be about $5 to $10 per person, then 100 guests will cost between $500 and $1,000, and when all the extra expenses are included, often more. If you have only so much money to work with, it seems at first glance that you have to decide if you want fewer guests and more food or more guests and less costly food. Yet other options are available. Since the reception is where the vast majority of your money is spent, there are other ways to trim costs without affecting the quality of your reception. (See the two "Reception" sections for examples.)

Aside from finances, there are other equally important decisions about the number of guests you want at your wedding. To a large degree, the number of people present determines what the atmosphere will be. For example, a small, intimate ceremony with about twenty-five close friends and relatives has a very different mood from a gathering of two hundred people. One question that needs to be answered is: What kind of wedding do we want? One that includes many friends and relatives, or one that is more private and perhaps more intimate? This is more a decision of taste and values than anything else.

Whatever size you finally agree on, the fact that you have determined who will be invited—that it is *your* feast day—is the important point. Your selection of friends and relatives (and your parents' suggestions, too) is a large part of what makes a wedding personal.

If you are planning on a wedding that will be out of the ordinary, you may begin to worry about how it will be received or accepted by older relatives or guests.

Many couples we spoke to were concerned about this. But in most cases the older guests were impressed, and said so. After all, they've been to more weddings than anyone else there and are therefore in a better position to appreciate any tasteful departure from tradition. Breaking traditions doesn't seem to matter much to most people—when they are replaced by newer traditions of a personal nature. So don't too readily change your own plans just because you think someone may be surprised, disappointed, or even shocked. Your fears are probably exaggerated. It's your day. Judging from all the people we spoke with, if your wedding is a true reflection of what you want to show the world, and you do it in a way that is considerate toward others, then it is highly unlikely that anyone will be offended if you break tradition.

OFFICIANT: Who officiates at a wedding planned by the couple themselves? In the late 1960s, some couples found it difficult to find members of the clergy who would go along with their plans. Unfortunately, many people had the impression that unlicensed, hippie gurus were the only ones blessing these new-style weddings. But the times, and people's opinions, have changed rapidly. When many of the country's major church organizations rewrote their marriage liturgies at the beginning of the 1970s, the majority of priests, ministers, and rabbis went along with the changes. So in most cases today, ordained, licensed clergy are the officiants at alternative weddings.

We have heard from a few couples who have told

us, in effect, "We planned our own wedding, then went to our minister and he said he wouldn't officiate unless we changed the whole thing and did it the normal way." This does happen sometimes. If you think you may encounter such a problem, get in touch with whomever you want as your officiant and make an appointment to talk over your plans. Most people have reported that unless a plan was too far-out or a particular officiant was especially conservative the minister, priest, rabbi, judge, or justice of the peace was willing to help them out more often than not.

First find out if the person you want to officiate is open to your ideas, and if so, set a date for the wedding. Do it long enough in advance, too. Some clergy are committed for months in advance.

But what if the person you want won't go along with your plans? We advise you to look for someone else who may be more sympathetic and in touch with your ideas. Don't let one person stand in your way—you can always find another officiant. It is important to find someone who will be in accord with you on your wedding day, not just standing there with you, mouthing the phrases.

If you do not want a religious ceremony, perhaps you can find a member of the clergy who is willing to dress in regular clothes and use only those secular parts of the ceremony that you have all agreed upon. Otherwise, you'll have to find a secular authority with the legal right to officiate at a wedding—usually a judge or justice of the peace (unless you decide to be married aboard ship, in which case the ship's captain may qualify). The legal aspect is important. If a wedding is performed by someone not recognized by your state, then, in the eyes of the law, you are not legally married.

Finally, try to choose someone who has known one or both of you, if this is possible. It can make things much simpler and much more intimate. But whomever you choose, engage the person early and talk together about your plans. He or she will probably have many good suggestions to offer, since anyone who has officiated at several weddings has had more experience than the average couple getting married.

You should almost always expect to give a fee or gift to your officiant. It can vary from $10 up to $100 (although $25 to $50 is the normal range), and depends in part on how much planning or rehearsal is involved. Find out what the fee is beforehand. Traditionally, on the wedding day, the fee, if it is in cash, is placed in a plain envelope, and the best man gives it to the officiant after the ceremony is completed. But this tradition is broken as often as it is followed, and you can pay the officiant in any way that feels comfortable for you.

RECEPTION—EARLY PLANNING: In traditional weddings, planning the reception usually takes more time, effort, and creativity than planning the ceremony does. In personal weddings, the balance usually shifts to a greater emphasis on planning the ceremony. But whatever type of wedding you have—from the most traditional to the most individualistic—if you plan on having a reception you'll want to give yourselves as much time as needed to plan it well. While the list of items may look long, arranging a smooth-running, enjoyable feast is not as hard as it looks at first. We discuss other aspects of the reception later on, but some answers you'll want to determine very early.

1. How much can you spend?

Your budget requirements will dictate many of your other decisions, so try to have a firm idea of your reception budget. If you can afford a lot of money, then your problems are minimized; if not, you'll find ways to cut corners without spoiling anything. Some people get their guest list in hand and figure out how much per person they will be able to spend—$5, $10, $25, etc. Others know from the start how much they are willing or able to spend; so their question becomes how to feed and entertain the guests for that amount of money. Either way, with this information, you'll be able to plan realistically.

2. Where will the reception take place?

Planning for a site shouldn't be too difficult, if you have left enough time. If the season is right, you might want to have the party outdoors, perhaps in someone's garden or backyard, or maybe at a friend's home. You can usually rent rooms of all sizes for receptions, but the costs can be very high. The main point is to find a site that is pleasant and warm in atmosphere, one that you like, and one that is large enough to accommodate your guests. If you are going to have dancing, keep in mind the amount of extra space needed. As with the wedding, a place that has some special meaning to you will be far more enjoyable than an unfamiliar place. Look around and find the best spot.

If you plan an outdoor reception, remember you'll

need chairs, tables, or other necessary equipment. If you have to rent any of this, make the arrangements far in advance.

3. What kind of food will you serve?

The answer to this question will be determined by your budget and by the time of day or night the reception takes place; and, of course, by your own tastes. Reception food can be very simple or very elaborate—there is no right or wrong. If caterers are handling your reception, meet with them early enough to make specific decisions on *exactly* what will be served and what the costs will be. Watch out for the "extras." If friends and relatives are taking care of your plans, make sure there is enough food for the number of guests, and enough help to prepare it and clean up.

4. What kind of beverage or liquor?

Most people attending a wedding reception expect some kind of spirits. But this, too, is a decision of taste and values. And money. Liquor can cost as much as food if you run an open bar. If you are opposed to having a lot of alcohol around, you can serve a punch or wine. There are numerous ways of handling this question, and they are discussed more fully later.

5. What do you do for a wedding cake?

If you're having caterers, they can usually provide a wedding cake. If you are not, bakeries often want a good deal of time to prepare something special like a wedding cake. If you plan to order a cake yourselves, give the bakery about one month's notice, especially if you are having a fancy one.

6. What do you want for music?

If you are going to have live music, arrange for the

person or group far enough in advance so you're sure to get them. Costs vary enormously for live music; be sure you set the price beforehand. If you don't want to hire live music, several of your guests probably have some musical talent and would be glad to play. Records and tapes can fill in very well, too. Try to get a good mixture of music since you'll probably have people of all ages and tastes at the reception.

7. *What do you do for help?*

If you're planning most of the wedding and reception yourselves, as most who have personal weddings do, then you'll need help at various points, especially on the wedding day. Parents and relatives are almost always willing to go out of their way to give assistance. You can ask friends to do certain chores that will lighten your load. If you're having a best man and maid of honor, ask them to take care of some things. By asking people to help you, you involve them in your plans and in your dreams. This is one of the greatest sources of joy that couples feel on their wedding day —that their friends are really happy for them, and with them.

INVITATIONS

Designing or making your own wedding invitations is one way of setting the tone for your wedding. How the invitation looks and what it communicates will begin to convey immediately whatever it is that is unique about your wedding, that distinguishes it from all others.

In formal, traditional weddings, the bride's parents announce the marriage, with their names at the top of the invitation. The form and the look of these invitations varies little. But in personal weddings it is most often the couple who are instrumental in planning the affair; and in a great many examples that we've seen, the invitations have come from them personally, not from the bride's parents. In other cases, the couple and their parents have designed invitations jointly, with beautiful results.

For many couples, the reason they broke away from the traditional invitation was because they had lived away from home for many years and did not feel their parents had much to do with their important decisions any longer. Another reason is expressed by one young woman who said, "I didn't like the old idea of my parents' 'giving me away' in any form. The wedding was ours so we announced it." Another wrote, "The formal invitation is so stuffy—we planned a casual, relaxed wedding, so we wanted invitations that would reflect that mood." Whatever the reason, invitations for alternative-style weddings are usually colorful, festive, or simple—or some combination of these.

Here are some ways couples have found to invite their friends and relatives to their weddings. The examples generally fall into two categories: (1) those invitations printed professionally, but containing either photographs, art work, or wording that make them unique, and (2) those invitations, hand printed, mimeographed, or done in some style other than the professionally printed announcements. In all cases, the formal wording was rejected for a more personal message—sometimes poetry, song lyrics, a printed letter of invitation, or a separate note to each guest.

1. One invitation to a wedding in a park contained three dittoed pages. The first page included the invitation given below; the second included a statement of the couple's commitment to each other; and the third included a map of roads leading to the wedding location.

"TWO ROADS CONVERGE IN A YELLOW WOOD"
—Please join us in our Celebration—
1:00 P.M. Sunday, October 8, 1972
Bring a friend, a pet, some music or poetry,
and some food to pass.
"very informal"
Please be with us.
Charlene and Al

2. On many invitations, the couple include a design, drawing, or photograph which has special meaning to them.

3. One invitation we saw had a bright red and yellow design on the front, with the word "LOVE" woven subtly into the design. As you open the invitation, in addition to the names of the couple's parents and the place and time of the wedding and reception, these words appear, followed by the couple's names.

We've uncorked it slowly and
inhaled the aroma;
We've taken a small sip . . .

Suddenly we've found
   ourselves transported
   into a strange
   and wonderful world . . .
   a world of Love.

We invite you to share
in our celebration of
this Love, as we are
united in marriage.

4. Another invitation has a woodcut of two faces on the front. Again, in addition to the particulars on the wedding, the inside of the invitation contains a few words of the couple's choosing.

for i have opened
                unto you
   the wide gates
        of my being

5. An old German custom has a representative of the bride's family go from house to house in the town, calling upon the guests to formally invite them to the wedding. Dressed in tie and tails, he knocks upon each door. When the door is opened, he removes his tall hat and asks all who are to be invited in that household to step into the parlor. When they are assembled there, he recites for them a memorized speech in which he gives all the details of the wedding and also tells a bit about the bride and groom and their parents.

This old custom has possibilities for many modern adaptations. Invitations could be personalized, over the telephone. In situations where the guests live in close proximity to the couple or their parents, the invitations could be delivered in person.

6. Many couples have written their invitation by hand.

Whatever invitation a couple or family decides upon, the message is the same. Come to *our* wedding, not the same wedding you've attended a dozen times before. Couples seem less and less satisfied following the convention of the printing industry and more and more enthusiastic about beginning their personal wedding from the moment they announce it. We know of no more graphic example than the following, a wedding invitation duplicated on a photocopying machine and sent out by a couple in Massachusetts.

TO OUR FRIENDS,

In writing this letter our intentions are many, one of which is to express our need for your understanding and commitment to our wedding. Our wedding is both common and unique—common in that the ceremony is a public affirmation of our values and ritualistic. It is unique in that it is happening to us at this time in our lives and that we have our own personal expectations for it.

Your understanding and commitment to our wedding can best be expressed in a feeling of community that we hope to create among those who come to the

wedding. Each of you who attends our wedding has a
special meaning to us and it is our hope that you will
get to know each other and share a part of yourselves,
your own uniqueness. And in sharing our expectations
for openness and informality we hope that you will come
to expect that our wedding will be a meaningful and
joyous experience for you and not just something you
have to do.

Trying to create a community has led us to think
about our wedding in certain ways. We chose the church
in Deerfield and the Inn because of their historic and
traditional setting, which reflects our ideas about ritual,
and also because of its worn comfortableness, soft chairs,
and ambiance. Our families will be staying there and
we'd like as many of our out-of-town friends to stay
there as possible.

Both of us feel that at most weddings a feeling of
community is not created because people don't have
enough time with each other. We would like you to
come as early in the week as you can or want to; on
Saturday friends here in this area have offered their
house and land for a barbecue, singing, dancing, guitar
playing . . . even the people here in Amherst don't get
together often enough and we'd like our wedding to be
one of the occasions when they do so.

Lastly, we would like people to participate in the
ceremony itself. We haven't invited people to be in our
wedding because we want everyone who comes to feel
equally special and involved. An idea we have is that
we'd like to have people read something during the
ceremony that is reflective and expressive of their
thoughts about marriage.

What more can we say except we hope that you'll come—caring, open, joyous, expectant, as we are now.

LOVE,

Bill and Kris

You may want to consider doing your own invitations by hand, including some kind of art work—maybe your own; choosing a format that you especially like, even though it is different from the usual; having an artist design it for you; using unusual colors; including a favorite message or poem on the cover or inside. There are also small shops in different cities that specialize in different kinds of invitations. If you're looking for more examples than provided here, see if there is a shop near you.

Be sure all the necessary information is on or with your invitation. Aside from your names, the date, time, and location of the ceremony, you may want to include a line about dress, so that no one is confused. You'll also want some indication of how many people will attend your reception, so an RSVP for the reception (and sometimes the wedding) is a good idea. If you are planning on doing anything unusual about gifts, this would be an appropriate time to convey whatever your wishes are.

DRESS

Often the most obvious way of distinguishing a personal wedding from a traditional one is the way the bride and groom and guests are dressed. Personal weddings tend to be more casual—brides often forgo buying one special dress, and grooms exchange formal garb for an open neck shirt or jacket and tie. But appearances can also be deceiving. Dressing in unconventional clothes or costumes does not automatically mean the wedding is intrinsically different from a traditional ceremony. The spirit of the ceremony and reception is what matters and what makes these weddings very different—not just the outward signs.

In a majority of personal weddings we've seen and heard of, dress was not an important issue; the bride, groom, wedding party, and the guests simply wore what was comfortable for them. There were no strict guidelines or rules, as there are for formal and semiformal weddings, where everyone is *expected* to dress in certain conventional garb. The real difference between the two types of wedding is that personal ceremonies leave everyone free to dress in a manner that is natural and comfortable. As a result, at the same ceremony you might see one man wearing bermuda shorts and another wearing a suit. Because what people wear is not an issue, no one needs to be worried about being "properly" dressed. What is happening at the wedding itself is the real concern.

In planning your wedding, you should decide how you feel about the dress question, decide how you, the couple, will want to dress, and then let your wedding party and guests know what to expect. If you want your guests to dress as they wish, you could let them know in the invitations or in a separate note. That way, no one will be surprised.

There are several advantages in dispensing with dress codes. First, you are free to wear what you want; you can express yourselves in your appearance as well as in your actions and words. Second, it eliminates the requirement that the groom wear a tuxedo or some other formal dress and the bride make or buy a special gown that is usually worn only once and then left hanging in the closet. In this respect, wearing what you want can cut down on expenses in a very big way. Third, your guests will be free to dress comfortably, and as a result they will probably be more relaxed and able to enjoy themselves. No one likes to be forced by convention to be uncomfortable.

Some people fear that the guests will show up in dirty dungarees if they are told to dress as they wish. It just doesn't happen that way. When the invitation or verbal request asks them to "Dress any way you will feel comfortable," they do dress differently, but they invariably show respect and sensitivity for the occasion and for what it means to the couple and their families.

We have heard of many different outfits worn by the bride and groom at their wedding—long robes, matching outfits, blue jeans, bathing suits, jump suits, wet suits, right on down to a couple getting married in the nude. To each his or her own. But in most cases, brides simply wear a favorite dress or suit and grooms wear a suit or sport jacket, or perhaps a sweater or open necked shirt. At outdoor weddings, often the range of dress is even greater.

We know of several weddings where the couple being married and some or all of the guests dressed around a certain "theme." At one very expensive and elaborate Chicago wedding in 1972, the couple asked guests to come dressed in attire from the 1890s, the 1930s, or the year 2001. At a Michigan ceremony, the ushers, best man, and groom all dressed in Abe Lincoln attire—tall stovepipe hats, long coats with tails, and full beards. We were not able to learn what purpose was intended by this dress. Perhaps the thought was to out-traditionalize the traditionalists.

So the choice is up to you; you set the standards because it's your wedding. Decide what dress codes, or lack of them, you want, and let your guests know. If you say nothing about dress, your guests might easily follow the traditional rules that determine "proper" dress for the time and place your wedding is being held. That is, if you are having an evening wedding, you might find some formally dressed guests who probably would have dressed otherwise had they known.

GIFTS

This would hardly seem to be an area where couples have many alternatives to consider. The matter of gifts is one those invited to a wedding usually determine for themselves. Depending on their sensitivity to the couple's needs and tastes, their own budget, the amount the couple or couple's family once spent on *their* wedding gifts, their desire to impress the parents of the couple, or other considerations, guests usually decide for themselves how much they will spend and what they will buy. Nevertheless, it is customary for the bride to register at a particular store the couple's preference for china, silverware, or glass. In that way, relatives and friends can each give one place setting or in some other way combine their individual presents into a larger gift which they know the couple wants and can use over many years. The custom makes a lot of sense.

Many couples, however, are uncomfortable with this traditional manner of gift giving. Some say they already have more than they need in the way of material things. Others are concerned about the ability of some of the guests to afford wedding presents. Others want to avoid getting themselves into a situation where they feel obligated to reciprocate on similar occasions in the future, preferring to give gifts when they are moved to and not because it is expected.

Gift-giving is a volatile issue, however. Some people genuinely enjoy giving gifts. Others find it about the only way they can communicate their love and concern. To deprive them of that opportunity can cause sadness or resentment.

Given all these pros and cons, many couples have still chosen alternative routes on the issue of gift-giving. Here are some of the methods employed.

1. A frequently used approach is to respectfully ask guests not to give presents. Sometimes the couple explain their reasons, sometimes they do not. In either

case the request always goes on or with the invitation, so the guests know, right from the start, what the norm will be.

2. Some couples ask certain guests, or all the guests, to bring something necessary for the wedding. Several guests might be asked to bring flowers, others food, others music, others drinks, others decorations, and so on. In this way, the couple and family reduce the cost of the wedding and the guests get the pleasure of giving and the genuine feeling of participation.

3. Some couples ask their guests to take the amount they would have spent on a gift and to give it, in the couple's name, to some charity or cause the guest would like to support.

4. Some couples make a list of charities or causes they would like to support, and send this list to the guests with the same request.

In following this alternative, it would be wise for the couple to include a variety of worthwhile causes or charities. Otherwise, the guests might feel resentful being asked to support organizations whose work they do not believe in. Having a varied list (political causes, medical research, etc.) gives every guest the chance to find at least one to support gladly.

5. Some couples have requested that their guests bring only gifts they have made themselves. This might make many guests uncomfortable at first; but the process of asking "What can I make? I haven't made anything in years. What could I make for them?" often turns out to be a stimulating one for the guests and finally results in gifts that have considerable meaning to both the giver and receivers. Sometimes the gifts

turn out to be small or crude. Sometimes guests throw themselves into making the gift, and an attractive piece of furniture, weaving, or art work is the result. In either case, the feeling is the same—the joy of giving one's own time, energy, and talent; the pleasure of receiving such a personal offering.

One couple we know asked their parents to give the following statement to any friends and relatives who asked "What do they *need?*" We include their *specific* alternatives to convey just how this approach works, but of course you would want to drop or add any items and insert the causes, charities, books, etc., of your own choosing.

Birth, christening, confirmation, Bar Mitzvah, Christmas, graduation, and wedding—all these occasions mark the beginning of something new—a new life, new roles and responsibilities, a new relationship. It is a tradition in our culture to celebrate these festive times with the giving of gifts. While this tradition of ritualized gift-giving provides a helpful channel for the sharing of love and care and hope, there are many forms which the spirit of giving can take.

If you feel you would like to give us a gift on the occasion of our forthcoming wedding, we sincerely appreciate your thoughtfulness. But since we have so much already, we would like to suggest some alternative means of gift-giving. Rather than buying us a present, here are several options we hope you will consider.

1 Donate some money to cancer research at the University of Minnesota. The name and address are:

"Cancer Research," Gift Receiving, Room 2598, 2610 University Ave., St. Paul, Minnesota 55114.

2 Buy yourself a subscription to *National Wildlife* magazine and write us a letter describing your impressions of the first issue you receive. We plan on living in the Adirondack Mountains of northern New York State and care deeply about the preservation of the environment. *National Wildlife* is one of the best and most beautiful of the environmental journals. Their address is: National Wildlife Federation, 1412 Sixteenth St., N.W., Washington, D.C. 20036. Subscription price is $6.50.

3 Do something you've been wanting to do which is new for you. After you've done it, write us a letter and tell us about it.

4 Spend some time doing something which you think will help promote world peace. Then write us a letter and share with us what you've done.

5 During the next many years, we will be working together as the Directors of the Adirondack Mt. Humanistic Education Center in Upper Jay, N.Y. AMHEC is a non-profit educational conference and resource center, devoted to helping educators, parents, and helping-professionals learn new methods and cultivate new skills. We are planning to expand both our buildings and programs over the next few years. A donation to AMHEC will help us reach more people in an increasingly effective way. The address is: AMHEC, Springfield Rd., Upper Jay, N.Y. 12987.

6 Send us a tape of your favorite songs and/or poems.

7 Write a poem, play, or story for us.

8 Paint us a picture—or make a collage, poster, etc.

9 Send us a few of your favorite recipes.

10 Here are some of our favorite books. It would be a real gift if you would read one that you haven't read before and write us a letter with your reactions.

Carl Rogers. *On Becoming a Person.* nonfiction.

Bertrand Russell. *Human Society in Ethics and Politics.* nonfiction.

Ken Kesey. *One Flew Over the Cuckoo's Nest.* novel.

E. E. Cummings. *100 Selected Poems.*

Henry David Thoreau. *Walden.* nonfiction.

Joseph Heller. *Catch-22.* novel.

Antoine de St. Exupery. *The Little Prince.* a beautiful fable.

A. S. Neill. *Summerhill: A Radical Approach to Child Rearing.* nonfiction.

OTHER IMPORTANT ARRANGEMENTS

By now, you've probably determined where, when, and what time your wedding will be held; you've arranged for someone to officiate, and you have a good idea of the kind of reception you will have. Those are the first, major arrangements and decisions. Now you can think about some of the other necessary items in your prewedding planning. For most of them you'll have dozens of alternatives open to you, ways to make your wedding more personal and unique. Here are these later, important arrangements:

ATTENDANTS: The tradition of selecting a best man and maid of honor dates back to ancient times. For some it was a matter of needing protection; but during the period when brides were openly considered property being transferred from one man to another, attendants served as helpers and legal witnesses. For the past hundred years and more the best man has helped do chores for the groom and the maid of honor has assisted the bride with her numerous arrangements and duties. The help was almost always needed—sometimes just to get the couple to the church altar. Today, one of the primary functions of the two friends asked to be primary attendants is usually to sign the marriage certificate with the officiant, thus making the marriage legal in the eyes of the State.

Because of tradition, most couples choose a best man and maid of honor for their wedding. It is a way of involving close friends directly in the proceedings. Recently, however, we have seen another, very popular alternative to this custom. Instead of choosing two friends for these special roles, many couples have decided instead to regard everyone present as their "Best People," thereby involving all guests in full participation at their wedding. The couple is joined by everyone at the altar, or everyone stands or sits in some arrangement that makes all feel equally involved. No one is singled out as more special than another. If ushers are needed, two or three friends can help guests find seats or a place to stand.

Thus in numerous personal weddings we have heard about even this ancient custom has been redefined because the couple desired the equal participation of everyone present. In most cases, guests have felt more involved and even closer to the bride and groom by sharing in their experience. For legal purposes, two guests were asked to sign the papers witnessing the marriage. And in terms of help, the couples asked many friends to pitch in on specific small duties, there again involving more of their guests. With many friends and relatives helping, things went very smoothly on the wedding day.

Your own plans and values will dictate whether or not you choose a maid of honor and best man. If you do, it is traditional for the couple to give each friend a small gift as a token of remembrance and thanks. Here you have many alternatives, and some of the best we've heard of have been gifts that were made by the couple or ones with a very personal meaning. Sometimes wedding photographs are given, or other tokens from the wedding day (but not the extra coffee pot given the couple by Uncle Roy and Aunt Clara). In any event, your gift should signify your thanks for their love and help on a very special day.

In the same way that couples have generalized the roles of best man and maid of honor, they have re-defined the roles of ushers, bridesmaids, and flower girl. Several children, and not necessarily girls, may hold or hand out flowers, distribute programs, and help out in small ways. And many more friends and relatives can be invited to participate in the ceremony (see the section called Participation) or help with the arrangements. The goal seems to be to make as many people as possible feel special and involved, rather than singling out a select few.

RINGS: Buying a wedding ring, or rings, is usually no problem; there are hundreds of designs and styles available and as many prices. Plain gold bands are the most popular rings nowadays; but like all fashion, this one is subject to swift change. Whether the groom chooses to wear a wedding band has long been a personal decision; there are no traditional guidelines governing his choice. Recently, many brides have adopted the same option.

Among couples having alternative weddings, we found a great number who chose to have their ring or rings designed and made by friends or acquaintances who were talented silversmiths. Many people are working professionally in handcrafts today, and they are usually very helpful if you have a special design in mind. Most are able to make any kind of ring you may want. If you are not impressed with the rings available at jewelry stores, try to find a metalsmith who can do the job for you. Very often the cost is comparable to, or lower than, what you would pay in a store. You will probably want rings of high quality workmanship and materials; remember, they should last a lifetime.

Not everyone chooses to have a ring. A large number of men and a smaller but growing number of women decide to do without them. Their reason may be simple—they don't like to wear rings; or they may not like the symbolism of the ring—that of captivity or possession; or they may not want to spend $50 to $500 for rings—either because they can't afford it or because it seems wasteful and unnecessary to them. If you have any question about whether or not you want to wear a ring, these are some of the issues you'll probably want to discuss.

But if you do decide to have a ring or rings, and if you decide to have it or them handmade, our advice is to find a metalsmith who uses fine materials, look at samples of his or her work, and make certain you like the design well enough. Be sure to give yourselves ample time, too.

PHOTOGRAPHERS: A good alternative to hiring a commercial photographer for your wedding is to have a friend photograph the wedding for you. There are several advantages to this. First, a friend knows you better. He or she will know what expressions are natural and common, what you like, and what pictures will be most valuable to you. Second, the cost of many commercial photographers is extremely high, even if their prints are excellent. A good friend with a good camera and some experience will probably be able to put together a beautiful book of photos at considerably less cost—or, if the photographer uses the pictures as a wedding present, at no cost to you at all. We've seen handsome wedding books put together by amateur photographers who really know their hobby, and because they were friends of the bride and groom, went all out to give them a fine book of pictures. Remember, however, that you will be asking your friend for a considerable gift of talent, time, and money.

Another alternative is to have someone take motion pictures at your wedding and reception. This is being done more and more these days. Motion picture equipment is easy to use (Super-8 and even 16mm), and although the price is higher than still photography, you will have a lasting record of your wedding and all who attended. As with still photographs, you can undoubtedly find a friend who will be willing and able to take the pictures. It is a good idea to get a rundown on the costs beforehand, however; motion pictures can be very expensive, especially if you want much footage shot. For either motion or still photography, find someone early, fix the costs, and above all make sure he or she is reliable. Although you may not require perfection, you don't want your pictures ruined by someone who is just beginning.

TAPE RECORDINGS: Most couples having personal weddings go to a good deal of work selecting passages, poems, and prayers to be read. And since the work really means something to them, and since their wedding really is unique and very special, they often want to preserve it by tape recording the ceremony. We have found few instances of this being done in traditional weddings, where the couple says very little during the whole service. But because personal weddings are based on what the couple wants to say, and often the thoughts and feelings of the participants celebrating with them, what is said is different and worth preserving. Making a tape is a relatively simple operation. Simply set up a tape recorder near you and ask someone to watch the controls to make certain the voice level is correct and to change the reels if necessary. Taping is much less expensive than photography. The blank tape costs no more than a few dollars. Thousands of couples do this each year, and so have a constant way to refresh their memories of their wedding. Along with photographs or motion pictures, a tape recording is a valuable record of the day.

FLOWERS: Flowers are usually considered an essential part of any wedding, whether winter or summer, indoors or out. Each season and each section of the country has its special flowers, so it is usually easy to choose between the many possibilities. Many flowers symbolize different feelings or states of mind. Traditionally, roses are the flowers of love, blossoms symbolize fertility, and lilies stand for purity.

Customarily, flowers are used in three different ways: those that are carried or worn, those used to decorate the wedding site, and those used at the reception. None of these is obligatory; many couples use a few flowers at the ceremony and none at the reception—it's all a matter of taste. Obviously, if you are having an outdoor wedding the need for cut flowers is greatly minimized; but even for most indoor affairs, flowers can be used sparingly and beautifully.

Many people don't think of flowers as a major expense, but if you don't look for an inexpensive way of supplying flowers for your wedding you can be very badly fooled. If you buy from a florist, be sure to get an exact estimate for executing your floral ideas, whether they are elaborate or simple. In many New York hotels, the flowers for the reception alone can run from $5,000 to $10,000. That's enough for the down payment on a house; yet sometimes unsuspecting couples are presented with a bill this size just for cut flowers and arrangements. These are extreme examples, of course, but they make an important point: check the costs carefully and do it far enough in advance to make alternative plans in case you find the rates too high.

Depending on your love for flowers and your feelings about being surrounded by them on your wedding day, floral expenses can seem very reasonable or very high. In the majority of personal weddings we know of, the couples did not spend a great deal on flowers. They found other tasteful ways of using flowers without spending hundreds of dollars purchasing flowers through a florist. Here are some of the ideas we've heard from others who have had to face this problem:

1. Bring flowers from the country if you're having an indoor wedding. Ask friends to help you gather common wild flowers, and you'll be able to cover a room at little or no expense.

2. Use a great deal of greenery instead of cut flowers. Greenery is very inexpensive compared to cut flowers, and used correctly, it is very beautiful.

3. Use flowers at the ceremony only and don't worry about the reception. Or the opposite: since people will be at the reception longer than at the wedding ceremony, concentrate the floral arrangements at the reception.

4. Carry the flowers from the wedding to the reception. This is done quite often; it's an easy way of keeping flowers around without spending double the money.

5. Use other decorations in place of flowers. (See the section below.)

6. Instead of carrying an elaborate bouquet, the bride can carry a single long-stemmed rose or a small spray from the garden or fields. A single rose looks

elegant and costs a fraction of the price of a bouquet. If the bride has attendants, they can do the same.

7. The bride can wear a few flowers in her hair instead of carrying them. Again, fewer flowers are needed.

8. Whatever custom is followed, the bride should choose flowers that are special to her. Like everything else at the wedding, the flowers chosen should be favorites. A few special flowers are likely to be appreciated more than a roomful of flowers that have no personal value.

9. If corsages are carried, it is customary to give one to the bride's mother and one to the groom's mother. The same applies to boutonnieres for the men.

In the end, these decisions will depend on your budget and tastes. Flowers are beautiful and almost always enhance the appearance of a person or a room; but how much is that appearance worth? If you plan carefully and look into the alternatives you'll probably be able to have enough special flowers without totally devastating your finances.

DECORATIONS: Flowers are only one type of decoration, and in traditional church weddings they have been considered the only type appropriate for the couple to introduce. But for outdoor weddings, and now increasingly in churches that are attempting to build into the physical setting a sense of the celebration of life, one has a great deal of latitude in modifying the environment. As is the case in all other aspects of your wedding, the space you create expresses your tastes and values and contributes to the atmosphere you want to achieve.

We have heard of all sorts of ways couples have altered or enhanced the physical setting of their wedding in a manner that was consistent with the words to be said and the actions to take place there. Here are some of the alternatives:

1. Posters or banners on the walls (or even hanging from trees) expressive of love, celebration, and reverence.

2. Favorite paintings or other art work placed, for the time, at the wedding site.

3. Different lighting effects such as partial lighting, dim lighting, candles, colored lights, etc.

4. Placement of chairs, platform, altar, tables—any of the physical arrangements that affect the way people interact, the way they relate to the couple during the ceremony. The tendency we have seen most often has been to arrange the furniture in a way that maximizes participation and involvement.

5. Incense or scented candles.

6. Partitions—especially if a small wedding is to take place in a large room. The partitions can be made of wood or curtains or even artistic table cloths or bedspreads.

7. Removal of objects in the environment (art work, paraphernalia, etc.) that do not contribute to the mood and tone of the wedding.

8. Use of rugs or blankets at outdoor weddings, if people are to be seated on the ground.

So once you have chosen the location for your wedding and reception, you should begin to consider how you might modify that spot to best achieve your goals for the wedding. It may be that you make few or no changes. On the other hand, you may find all sorts of creative ways to give the physical area a personality of its own—one that is congenial to you and your guests on your wedding day.

Of course, if you are in a building or an outdoor area that does not belong to you, you'll want to check out any changes you have in mind beforehand. You don't want any last-minute surprises, like the custodian taking your banners down as the guests are coming in for the ceremony.

MARRIAGE LICENSE: This is an item about which you have no alternatives—if you want to be legally married, that is. Each state requires you to buy a license before you get married. Most states stipulate that both of you have a blood test as well. Laws and requirements vary from state to state, so the easiest way to find out the cost of the license and any blood test requirement is to call your local city or town hall and ask for the Marriage License Bureau. They will tell you what you must do, where to go, and the cost of all legally required procedures.

PRE-WEDDING PARTIES

Traditionally, a wedding is celebrated at several parties before the actual wedding day arrives. These parties take different forms; the usual ones are: (1) bridal showers, (2) stag parties for the groom, given by his friends, and (3) the bridal dinner, sometimes called the rehearsal dinner, given a night or two before the wedding. It is also common for friends of the couple to give parties in their honor or to invite them for dinner, although these do not fall into the three traditional categories above.

Bridal showers have been given traditionally by women friends of the bride, almost always for the purpose of gift-giving. A bride may be given one or two showers, but the number can range up to eight or nine. For obvious reasons, this can put an enormous strain on a close friend's gift-giving capacity. If the bride is not interested in collecting dozens of presents from friends and relatives in this fashion, she can try to limit the showers to one, or maybe even none. Many brides have said they felt uncomfortable collecting presents at showers. Their friends were "obligated" to bring a gift, and the brides would rather have not put them in the position of feeling that the showers were little more than forced gift-giving.

Male stag parties don't involve gifts; traditionally they are parties where close friends of the groom gather for "a last night with the boys," before heading to the altar. Often the stag is a "bachelor's dinner" that takes place a week or so before the wedding. Fathers of the bride and groom usually attend, and it is sometimes an occasion for male members of the families to get acquainted, in an informal way, before they become in-laws.

The bridal dinner is customarily held just before

the wedding; it is attended by relatives of the couple plus the wedding party. If a rehearsal is needed for the wedding, the dinner takes place after the rehearsal. Like all other parties, the main intention is honoring the couple.

These three types of parties are the traditional ones given before the couple's wedding. But like everything else covered in this book, many alternatives for festivities are being explored. Usually what is done to honor the prospective bride and groom depends on what their friends or relatives think up. It may be a party with a theme, or perhaps a get-together in the daytime, or perhaps a picnic. Many couples don't become involved in any of the traditional parties at all. They simply celebrate with their friends and relatives in the same ways they hope to celebrate with them after the marriage—by dining, dancing, singing, or through sports, or through any other occasion that brings friends and loved ones together.

But where pre-wedding parties do occur, they are usually part of the fun of getting married and help to create an expectation for the wedding itself.

PLANNING YOUR HONEYMOON

Finally, if you want to have a honeymoon, now is the time to start planning for it. We bring the subject up in prewedding planning simply because you will have to arrange for tickets, reservations, accommodations, and all the other necessities of travel ahead of time. If you're going abroad, you'll need up-to-date passports and health records—all well in advance of your departure. Wherever you plan on going, whether camping, touring, or just finding a nice place to be alone, be sure you make arrangements far enough in advance so your travel plans don't interfere with your wedding arrangements. It's usually a good idea to get the honeymoon plans over with as soon as possible, then spend your time deciding about the ceremony and reception. Otherwise, you're liable to find yourself in a last-minute rush in which all your plans fare the worse.

THE CEREMONY

Couples who plan traditional weddings generally don't spend much time beforehand thinking about the ceremony. There is little for them to do or say except to make their entrance, stand quietly, repeat the officiant's words, say "I do," exchange rings, and kiss each other. The nuptials are entirely in the hands of the officiant. The couple, waiting passively to say their lines, are rather like two people taking an oath of office. In this case, the most important part of the wedding day is, unfortunately, the one that commands the least attention, the least planning, the least creativity. Couples in traditional ceremonies have more or less abdicated their rights to determine how, and with what prayers, poems, vows, or contracts, they will be married. When the actual wedding ceremony is taken so much for granted, it is not surprising that people of all ages say that it has lost its meaning.

It is in the planning for and in the uniqueness of the ceremony itself that personal weddings differ most dramatically from traditional ones. What makes a wedding personal is not the surface changes—a wild reception, different dress, artistic invitations. In most personal weddings it is the ceremony, the celebration of marriage, that is the central focus of the couple's activities and planning—a wedding that is thought out by the couple and therefore becomes an extension of themselves. While other aspects of the whole wedding are important, it is in the ceremony that the deepest emotions are felt, the most abiding promises and declarations made. Those couples who break from past traditions and take the responsibility of building their own thoughts, wishes, and values into their ceremonies are the ones who really give meaning to a personal wedding.

Even with all the guests around, a wedding tends to be a very special, almost private affair for the couple; their thoughts often center on their own feelings and the feelings of their partner. Many couples get so wrapped up in the excitement, fear, nervousness, and joy of the event that they have little time to think about their guests—those called upon to witness the marriage. Yet weddings have also always been feasts, public celebrations, a time when a group of friends and relatives—or a whole community—gathers to rejoice. In the majority of traditional weddings, the couple is almost segregated from the guests until the reception. The ceremony is made of stock components, unchanged for many years, and it does not include much, if any, participation by the guests.

This is the other major difference between most traditional and personal weddings. In the latter, the couple usually *want* the involvement of the guests. In personal weddings, the emphasis is not so much on "performance" and "doing the right thing" as on achieving an atmosphere where everyone present feels part of the marriage by participating in the service. In writing their weddings, couples strive for the involvement of all present, so that the ceremony (rather than the reception) is the most memorable part of the wedding.

These ideas are not new. Interaction between the couple and their guests is an ancient custom. But when weddings became more "sophisticated," dictated by rules of church and state instead of the rules of the folk community, this important aspect seemingly was lost as an active element. The guests became mere observers, not real participants.

In these two areas of involvement, the couple's and the guests', the personal wedding is not so far-out or radical as some of its detractors (and even some of its supporters) have claimed. Couples celebrating personal weddings are adding many new elements, to be sure; but in reality they are reaching far back into history and reviving some of the most ancient and honored customs that surround the marriage rite. "Something old, something new"—the phrase takes on new meaning for the couples planning their own ceremonies. They are borrowing respected rituals from the past, then adding elements unique to them—to their own experience of being alive, of feeling and loving in the present.

PROGRAMS

At many traditional weddings, a copy of the program is given to the guests as they enter. The programs usually include the order of events in the ceremony; the titles, composers, and musicians or soloist for any music; the names and roles of all the people in the wedding party; and, occasionally, a part of the traditional service. These programs help the guests follow the ceremony, especially if many songs are to be sung. They also serve as a permanent reminder of the occasion.

Many couples having personal weddings have followed this practice of distributing programs. And, as you would expect, their programs have differed in form and content. Since most alternative weddings are made up of at least some elements the guests are unfamiliar with—such as personal poems and new vows—programs help the participants feel more comfortable and able to follow the ceremony with ease. Numerous people commented to us that one of their goals in having a personal wedding was to involve everyone present in the entire ceremony. To do this, they gave every guest full copies of songs, prayers, poems, or other readings. In most cases, they said, when the people had a copy of a song or poem in their hands, they felt less inhibited and were more likely to take an active role.

Programs take many different forms. Some are professionally printed, some elaborately designed by artists, and some are mimeographed or photographically copied. Many couples go all out to make their programs attractive, since they feel that even the programs represent an essential part of their wedding.

If you choose to have a program, its content will depend on the elements you want to include in your ceremony. Some ceremonies are long, with numerous readings; some are very short. The general trend in preparing programs has been to print as much of the service as practical, directing the guests from one part to the next. When the couple wants the congregation to read aloud or sing, the program directs them to do so. It seems clear that planners of personal weddings usually have put so much care and love and artistry into their ceremony that they want to share it with everyone, and the program is a perfect way of achieving this end.

We have seen programs for all kinds of personal weddings. In one formal wedding, for example, the program was quite traditional ("Solo—O Perfect Love; Bride Given in Marriage by Her Father," etc.). But on the back of the program appeared a personal note by the bride and groom. It was short, but it was their own expression of their values, freely chosen for inclusion on their part.

We thank you for completing our joy with your presence as we are united in marriage. We are glad you could share in the outward expression of our feelings this evening. We hope you will also continually find yourself complete in Him.

For because of our faith, He has brought us into this place of highest privilege where we now stand, and we confidently and joyfully look forward to actually becom-

ing all that God has had in mind for us to be. (Romans
5:2, *The Living Bible*).

SINCERELY,

Rollie and Betty

The program at a wedding can also contain an ex-
planation of various parts of the service. One minister
in Kentucky wrote a fourteen-page booklet explaining
every element in the very traditional wedding service
at which he was married. This excerpt gives something
of its flavor.

> The flower girl is the last to process before the bride
> enters. Small children originally were brought into close
> association with the bride in the hope that through
> sympathetic magic she would be fertile. Small boys some-
> times were used in the same way to make the bride have
> male children. The main idea was that like produces like
> at times of so much holiness and power.
>
> Of course, this is not the reason that Susie Johnston,
> Karen's cousin, serves as our flower girl. On this date
> seventeen years ago, Karen was a flower girl in the wed-
> ding of Susie's parents, and we want to include Susie in
> ours. She represents one of the purposes of marriage—to
> bring children into the world and through the church,
> that our common Christian faith may find constant soil
> for growth and renewal.

For final examples, we want to include the entire
programs of two personal weddings—one in Duluth,
Minnesota, and one in New York City—changing only
the names, as has been our custom throughout this
book.

[The following program was composed for the wedding of Bob and Christine in Duluth.]

PRELUDE

Organ solo:	"Jesu Joy of Man's Desiring"	Bach
Vocal solo:	"Speak Softly Love"	Rota Kusik

PROCESSIONAL

"Air from Water Music Suite"	Handel
"Trumpet Tune in D Major"	Purcell

(Congregation, please remain seated.)

RITE OF MARRIAGE

Statements of our dependency upon human relationships:

(minister)

> If I truly love one person,
>   I love all persons,
>   I love the world,
>   I love life.
> If I can say to somebody else,
>   "I love you,"
> I must be able to say,
>   "I love you everybody,
>   I love through the world,
>   I love in you also myself."
>
> —Erich Fromm

> Man, however, is not a self-sufficient
>   separate entity,
> but is constituted by the things
>   he makes his own.

In every form of his being,
    man is related to something
other than himself.
If he makes himself the immediate object
    of his efforts,
he is on his last and perilous path;
    for it is possible,
that in doing so, he will lose
    the Being of the other
and then no longer find anything
    in himself.

                      —Karl Jaspers

Call to the community: (minister)

We've come this evening to share in the celebration of love between Bob and Christine. We are their friends and relatives, but we represent all of mankind. In realization of our binding relationship to them, and one another, let us all stand and sing this song, expressing the feelings of love and happiness that pass between us on this occasion.

Song: "Pass It On"   —Kurt Kaiser   (community)

It only takes a spark
To get a fire going.
And soon all those around
Can warm up in its glowing
That's how it is with God's love—
Once you've experienced it;
You spread His love to everyone;
You want to pass it on.

What a wondrous time is spring
When all the trees are budding.
The birds begin to sing,
The flowers start their blooming.
That's how it is with God's love—
Once you've experienced it;
You want to sing, It's fresh like Spring;
You want to pass it on.

What a wish for you my friend;
This happiness that I've found.
You can depend on Him,
It matters not where you're bound.
I'll shout it from the mountain top—
I want my world to know,
The Lord of love has come to me;
I want to pass it on.

Statement on the joy which accompanies love: (minister)

To love one who loves you
To admire one who admires you
In a word to be the idol of one's idol
is exceeding the limit of human JOY
It is stealing fire from heaven.

—Girardin

Cello solo: "Ode To Joy"   —Beethoven

Statement of belief in the possibility of fulfillment through marriage: (minister)

> That there should exist one other person in the world toward whom all openness of exchange should establish itself, from whom there should be no conceal-ment, whose body should be as dear to one, in every part as one's own; with whom there should be no sense of mine or thine, in property or possession; into whose mind one's thoughts should naturally flow, as it were; to know whom and oneself, there should be a spontaneous re-bound of sympathy in all the joys and sorrows and ex-periences of life; such is perhaps one of the dearest wishes of the soul.

—Edward Carpenter

Exchange of promises: (minister and couple)

MIN: Bob and Christine, having felt the joy which ac-companies your love for one another, and firmly be-lieving in the fulfillment of a lifetime together, do you take each other to be husband and wife?

BOB: I, Bob, take you, Christine, as my wife.

CHRISTINE: I, Christine, take you, Bob, as my husband.

MIN: Do you both promise to bring faith, hope, and joy to your marriage?

BOB: I promise to bring faith, hope, and joy to our marriage.

CHRISTINE: I promise to bring faith, hope, and joy to our marriage.

MIN: Will you both be consoling, understanding, and forgiving?

BOB: I will be consoling, understanding, and forgiving.

CHRISTINE: I will be consoling, understanding, and forgiving.

MIN: Will you love each other and give yourselves fully to each other as husband and wife?

BOB: Christine, I will love you and give myself fully to you as your husband.

CHRISTINE: Bob, I will love you and give myself fully to you as your wife.

Couple's prayer

Where there is hatred, let us sow love;   (couple)
where there is injury, pardon;
where there is doubt, faith;
where there is despair, hope;
where there is darkness, light;
and where there is sadness, joy.

Grant that we may not so much seek to be consoled,
as to console;
to be understood, as to understand;
to be loved, as to love;
for it is in the giving that we receive.

—Saint Francis

The giving of rings: (couple)

BOB: I give this ring to you as a symbol of my love and decision to continually renew my promises.

CHRISTINE: I give this ring to you as a symbol of my love and decision to continually renew my promises.

Call for response: (minister)

Bob and Christine have exchanged marriage promises. In the midst of their individuality, their person is one. We have witnessed their statements of love for one another. It is right for us, at this time, to respond to their witness.

Community response and promise: (community)

We, as a community, are glad to accept you in your new relationship to one another. You have responsibilities to each other, and to us, since your future actions will affect all of mankind. We, too, are responsible to you, in that you are a part of us, and our actions will greatly influence you. Just as you have promised to uphold your responsibilities to one another, and therefore, to us, we will uphold the responsibilities we have to you, and amongst ourselves. Let us celebrate our intent to be victorious in these responsibilities, and our happiness in the love you are sharing with us.

Vocal solo: "Sunrise, Sunset"   —Bock, Harnick

RECESSIONAL
"Theme from the Masterpiece Theater"   —Mouret

(Please remain seated until the ushers direct you out of the sanctuary.)

The bride and groom will be waiting to celebrate with you at the reception, downstairs, in the "Lakeview Social Hall."

[The following program was composed for the wedding of John and Sally in New York City.]

The Celebration of Marriage

FLOWERS
(Flowers symbolize the beauty of life.)

Medley of Hymns and Songs:

> Maryanne Jones, pianist
> Robert Morgan, bass

BELLS
(Bells symbolize the joy and excitement of life.)

Ringing of the bells in rhythm and harmony:

> Everyone

Poem: "The Bells" by Edgar Allan Poe

> Frank Isaac

Litany: Genesis 1

> WOMEN: In the beginning God created the heavens and the earth.
>
> MEN: And God said, let us make man in our image, after our likeness;
>
> WOMEN: And let them have dominion over the fish of the sea and over the fowl of the air, and over cattle.
>
> MEN: And over all the earth and over every creeping thing that creepeth upon the earth.

WOMEN: So God created man in his own image; in the image of God created he them.

MEN: And God blessed them, and God said unto them, Be fruitful, and multiply and replenish the earth.

UNISON: And God saw everything that he had made and behold, it was very good, and the evening and the morning were the sixth day.

Prayer of Invocation   Eleanor Bender
A Song from the Adam and Eve Duet from Haydn's "The Creation" arranged for Voice and Flute
                              Phyllis O'Hara, soprano
                              Loretta Nash, flutist

VEIL
(The Veil symbolizes the traditions of marriage)

Andrews Family History and Traditions

Mason Family History and Traditions

Pinning her mother's veil on Sally

FRUIT
(Fruit symbolizes all the pleasures of life.)

Litany: Song of Solomon

MEN: O my love, let me see thy countenance, let me hear thy voice, for sweet is thy voice and thy countenance is comely.

WOMEN: The voice of my beloved! Behold, he cometh

leaping upon the mountains, skipping upon the hills. My beloved is like a roe or a young hart.

MEN: For lo, my love, winter is past, the rain is over and gone; the flowers appear on the earth; the time of the singing of birds is come and the voice of the turtle is heard in our land.

WOMEN: As the apple tree among the trees of the wood, so is my beloved among the sons. I sat down under his shadow with great delight, and his fruit was sweet to my taste.

MEN: The fig tree putteth forth her green figs, and the vines with the tender grape give a good smell.

WOMEN: His left hand is under my head and his right hand doth embrace me. Awake, O north wind; and come, thou south wind, blow upon my garden that the spices thereof may flow out. Let my beloved come into his garden and eat his pleasant fruits.

MEN: Thy lips are like a thread of scarlet, and thy speech is comely. Thy lips are as the honeycomb, honey and milk are under thy tongue.

WOMEN: I sleep, but my heart waketh: it is the voice of my beloved that knocketh, saying, open to me.

UNISON: Many waters cannot quench love, neither can the floods drown it. Set me as a seal upon thy heart, as a seal upon thine arm, for love is strong.

Prayer of blessing: Frank Isaac

Sharing of the Fruit: Medley—Musicians

Hymn: "For the Beauty of the Earth"

For the beauty of the earth,
  for the glory of the skies,
For the love which from our birth
  over and around us lies,
Lord of all, to thee we raise
  this our hymn of grateful praise.

For the beauty of each hour
  of the day and of the night,
Hill and vale and tree and flower
  Sun and moon and stars of light.
Lord of all, to thee we raise
  this our hymn of grateful praise.

For the joy of ear and eye,
  for the heart and mind's delight.
For the mystic harmony
  linking sense to sound and sight.
Lord of all, to thee we raise
  this our hymn of grateful praise.
                                        Amen.

RINGS

(The rings symbolize the intention to be loving.)

Ringing of the Bells: Everyone

Scripture: 1 Corinthians 13
                                           Frank Isaac

Poem: "On Marriage"   from The Prophet
                                          by Kahlil Gibran
                                          Eleanor Bender

Rings:

John to Sally
Sally to John

Thoughts on Marriage: Frank Isaac

Declaration and Blessing: Eleanor Bender

FOOD AND DRINK
(Food and Drink symbolize community and sharing.)

Please help yourself and pass it along.

Singing and Guitar Playing   Judy Mitchell

Thoughts about Marriage (John):

I see our marriage as an attempt to crystallize from
our cultural and religious heritages those aspects of marriage which seem meaningful to our lives in New York
City, on June 5, 1971.

Some of the symbols of marriage are honored as echoes
of an ancient time when a social contract in marriage was
an advancement in human relationships in that the limita-
tions of the power and the responsibilities of a master for
his children, servants and wives was defined. Recognizing
that such a contract is not relevant to our ideals that "all
men and women are created equal and are endowed by
their creator with certain inalienable rights," we are seeking in marriage to celebrate our friendship, companion-
ship and love as independent, self responsible persons who

affirm each other's existence, right of opinion, freedom of thoughts and expression of affection.

Thoughts about Marriage (Sally):
I see our marriage as an affirmation of a commitment to the intention of being loving. By that I mean being present in the moment and paying attention lovingly, reverently and with good-will.

It means to listen and hear
            to understand and let be
It means individually to be in touch
            with our feelings and to express
            them appropriately
            to be accountable for our behavior
            to be responsible for our direction.

I expect that there will be those times when we will lose sight of our intention. I hope we will understand that love is there even when there is little evidence—that when we are angry and withdrawn, it is not so much that the other has failed but that the one has retreated to an island of security.

And I hope that if sometimes we move away from each other, that we can wait knowing that mutuality is a process that encompasses both light and shadow.

I trust that we will be able to discuss our differences as growing edges of creativity and stay near each other—that we can share our thoughts and feelings with openness and in a way that will enrich our time together.

I expect that our marriage will be, as our relationship

has been, a joyful sharing and a means for each of us to move into deeper individual awareness and fulfillment.

I trust too, as we enjoy the richness of life together, that we will be open to sharing with others.

These expectations and hopes arise from a faith in the infinite and cosmic resources of Love and Truth that I identify as God.

PROCESSIONAL

The traditional processional for a wedding dates back many centuries. The bride is escorted down the aisle by her father and then "given away" to her new husband at the altar. When men were still buying wives, this custom had some meaning—the father was turning over his "property" to the buyer. The woman was not only considered property; she was also escorted and "given" to the new man to insure that there was no break in her dependence on men and servitude to them.

This ritual has lasted as part of the traditional wedding even after brides ceased to be bought and sold. But women today are finding the custom repugnant. They don't want to be treated as chattel, even symbolically.

The different approaches to the processional in personal weddings are very interesting. Couples have tried to find ways that have new meaning, without demeaning either partner. Here are a few of the ways couples have solved the problem:

1. After the guests are seated, the couple walks to the altar together, unescorted.

2. Both parents escort the bride down the aisle, but the father does not "hand over" the bride at the altar. This preserves the closeness felt in families on a wedding day; the family comes in together, but the giving away aspect is dropped. (Similarly, the groom's parents could escort him down the aisle.)

3. The bride and groom are inside the church or house before any guests arrive. As the guests come in, the couple and their families mingle among them, help them get seated, and so on. This reverses the usual custom and creates a setting in which the couple is doing the welcoming. It does away with the need for ushers. And, more important, it helps diminish the nervousness that couples experience when they feel they are performing in a grand entrance.

4. One couple slowly folk-danced down the aisle, greeting guests and pausing to say hello as they went.

5. One or several friends escort the bride to the altar to meet the waiting groom. Or the bride waits and the groom is escorted.

6. At outdoor weddings, processionals tend to be more casual; the couple usually greets the guests as they arrive. When everyone is present, the guests gather around the site of the ceremony. An exception to this style was found in upstate New York, at a boarding school. The couple, both teachers, arrived at their wedding in a buckboard drawn by horses. All their students, friends, and relatives were assembled beforehand.

7. In another outdoor ceremony, the guests assembled at the site by the shore of a lake, and the bride and groom canoed in to the dock to the ringing of bells.

8. One couple had a midnight wedding in a Philadelphia church. The church was totally dark, and as guests arrived they were given long, lighted candles and then escorted to pews. The bride and groom, carrying candles, then made their processional down the

aisle to the sound of African drum music. After the processional, the church lights were turned up and the wedding itself was traditional.

9. As in the previous example, candles often play a part in the processional and in the wedding. In another variation the bride and groom each carried a lighted candle to the altar. The minister had one unlighted candle which the bride and groom lit with theirs. They extinguished their own candles, and the "oneness candle" was placed on the altar.

10. In still another variation each guest was given an unlighted candle on entering and directed to a seat in a large circle. Two seats were left empty for the bride and groom. The lights were dimmed. After people fell quiet, the couple entered the room, each holding a lighted candle, and walked across the circle to their seats. Then each reached to the side and lighted the candle of the person next to them. Each of these people lighted another candle, and so on around the circle until everyone's candle was lighted.

In all of these processionals, the couples varied the traditional ritual not only to fit the mood of their wedding, but also to depart from the age-old association of a father's giving his daughter away. The processional begins the ceremony, and couples having personal weddings wanted to start their weddings on their own, as equals, and with some degree of uniqueness.

We should add that not all weddings have processionals as such. It is clearly one dramatic way to begin the ceremony, but it is certainly not the only way. Two further examples should illustrate this point.

11. At a wedding in Florida, the room was almost totally dark as the ushers guided guests to their seats. When everyone was present, the lights were completely extinguished. After a few moments, the silence was broken with the "Morning" theme from Grieg's "Peer Gynt Suite." Simultaneously, the light in the room was gradually increased and the wedding party could be seen already in their places up front. Also, for the first time the guests could see the beautiful decorations that filled the room. The effect was highly dramatic, although there was no movement from place to place.

12. In another wedding the lights were also dimmed when the guests were seated. Suddenly a spot light was thrown on the groom, seated to one side on a raised platform. With his guitar, he began to sing a song that he and the bride had chosen. On the second verse, a second spot illumined the bride, sitting on the opposite side of the room, who joined in the singing. (The couple being married need not sing or play instruments for this to work. They could read something instead.)

Processionals and similar beginnings are somewhat theatrical in nature. They help create a sense of excitement and added importance to the occasion. You may not want to have a highly dramatic opening; but some approach that conveys a clear sense of *beginning* is usually effective and well appreciated.

MUSIC AND SINGING

MUSIC: Think of any kind of music, and you can be sure it has been played at someone's wedding. Whether it is traditional church music, classical, rock, pop, Renaissance, opera, jazz, folk, or country and western—live, recorded, or electronically synthesized—we have heard of its use at personal weddings.

Music is a powerful way to contribute to the atmosphere you want to create. It is used in weddings the world over and throughout time. Ancient ceremonies were probably accompanied by flute players; drums have always been an integral part of African weddings. Music adds a dimension to any ceremony that cannot be achieved with words alone.

Traditional church organ music is used to create a serious, religious mood. Many choices are available. The most universal, traditional piece associated with weddings is the "Wedding March" from Wagner's "Lohengrin." It has been used for a hundred years to accompany the bride on her long walk down the aisle to the altar. But as we have found out, and as *Newsweek* Magazine reported (July 17, 1967), although Wagner's piece is still standard, "a growing number of couples consider 'Here Comes the Bride' as outmoded as the dowry." Numerous couples have looked elsewhere for their wedding music.

The easiest way to convey the joyousness of the occasion is to select music and songs that capture a sense of wonder and love. Here, too, there are abundant possibilities; and again, your tastes should dictate the choices.

If you want to have a wide variety of music, the tape recorder makes it very easy for you to select and record the music that is meaningful and expressive for you. Many couples have played music from the time their guests arrived, through the ceremony, and all through the reception, simply by programming the tapes in sequence and asking a friend to run the recorder. This method offers an unlimited choice of music, and it is easy and inexpensive, as well.

The other option, of course, is live music. Here again there are many ways to proceed. Some couples have printed the words to songs in their programs or on separate sheets so all the guests can join in. This has been a long-standing custom for religious hymns. Having guests participate in singing has usually been an effective way of involving them actively in the ceremony.

If you have friends or relatives who are musicians, you might want them to play selected pieces at the wedding. Recorders and stringed instruments tend to produce beautiful background music. Folk music is very popular, and one person is often enough for this type of accompaniment. We have also heard of couples hiring rock bands for their marriage rites. At one wedding where the groom was a member of a rock band, his group played music he had written especially for the ceremony. Another couple, being married with a traditional service in a large garden asked two friends who were talented in Renaissance music to play throughout the wedding. The classical sound matched the ceremony perfectly, and the combination was very moving. Another couple, both singers, sang a duet to each other at one point during their wedding, accompanied by friends who played various instruments.

There are still other possibilities. If poetry is being used, backing up the reading with one or two instruments can be very effective. Other couples have used bells during the service to create a sense of religious worship as well as a beautiful sound. One couple asked all the guests to bring small bells with them to the wedding; on the program each person received, the times were noted when everyone was to ring his or her bell during the ceremony. The church was filled with this joyous sound at various intervals throughout the service.

Whatever the choice of music or the way it is performed, couples having personal weddings have chosen pieces that have had some special meaning to them— either something they both loved, or music that seemed to fit the mood of their wedding. The more personal the music, the more both people seemed pleased with their choice.

SONGS: Couples who choose a few songs with words for their wedding very often use one piece to replace "The Wedding March" processional and another to be used at the recessional. Just as often, the songs are played and sung at key points during the ceremony. The soloist or singers may be professionals, friends, relatives, or, very often, one or both of the couple themselves.

Most often the music is happy, the lyrics are about love, and the effect is one of joy and celebration. Many of the people we talked with chose pieces of serious music—classical, Romantic, or modern—that they especially enjoyed. But we also found that a growing number of people continue to choose popular music to replace the old standards or conventional church music. Show tunes are popular, as are certain pieces by the Beatles, Simon and Garfunkel, individual folk singers, and a variety of groups. The list of songs could be endless, but we have room for only a few titles to suggest the many that have been used by people from all over the country. Some of the more popular ones have been:

> "Sunrise, Sunset" ("Fiddler on the Roof")
> "One Hand, One Heart" ("West Side Story")
> "All You Need Is Love" (Beatles)
> "Turn, Turn, Turn" (adapted from Ecclesiastes and set to music by Pete Seeger)
> "More" ("Mondo Cane")
> "We've Only Just Begun" (Carpenters)
> "Love Story"—theme
> "Both Sides Now" (Joni Mitchell)
> "Bridge Over Troubled Waters" (Simon and Garfunkel)
> "Wedding Processional" ("Sound of Music")
> "Let It Be" (Beatles)
> "The Wedding Song" (Buffy St. Marie)

Selecting one or more songs you love and working them into the ceremony is usually one of the most enjoyable parts of wedding planning.

PARTICIPATION

One of the most important goals for couples planning a personal wedding seems to be to insure participation. They want their friends and relatives to be involved in the wedding, just as they will be involved in the couple's ongoing married life.

Participation is a fundamental principle of marriage, dating far back into ancient times. In mystical societies, the relationship between the couple and their community was all-important. When religious doctrines took over as the dominant laws of marriage, the idea that the group was in ways "responsible" for the couple was firmly embedded. In order to achieve and perpetuate a community, friends, relatives, and particularly the community elders had to look out for the well-being of the novice couple. Thus, guests were not asked to a wedding only for the feast; they were present to witness the bonds and in turn promise their assistance to the couple to try and help them have a happy and satisfying life.

The concept of community responsibility seems almost to be lost in this country nowadays; it is noticeably absent in most traditional ceremonies, even in church weddings where the promise of community support is supposedly part of the service. Couples who have planned personal weddings have told us that it was the lack of participation in friends' weddings that started them thinking about ways to change the situation for themselves. They wanted to eliminate the feeling of alienation that they thought existed in many traditional weddings. Here are some of the ways couples have tried to involve their guests in the wedding celebration.

1. Many couples have arranged the physical setting of the ceremony so as to involve everyone by placing the guests in circles, semicircles, or in some other way close to the couple. This often means that everyone stands in contrast to the conventional arrangement in churches where the guests sit in rows of pews while the couple performs on stage. Changing the usual, physical make-up of a room can quickly change the entire atmosphere of the wedding.

2. In traditional services, the guests don't see the bride and groom until the actual ceremony, and they don't speak to them until the reception. As they watch the wedding, they often feel somewhat distant from the couple, whom they may not have spoken to for some time. A simple alternative to remedy this is to greet guests individually as they enter the site of the ceremony. This helps the guests to feel closer to the couple as they watch or participate in the service.

3. A woman from East Rochester, New York, recalls one aspect of a wedding she attended: "As each guest entered the chapel they were handed a wild flower by one of the bridesmaids. The flowers were held during the ceremony or used by the men as boutonnieres. It was a nice touch that made me feel I was a real part of the wedding and not just a spectator."

4. Joint readings and responsive readings are two of the oldest ways to involve participants or the con-

gregation in a service. In ancient times, chants or phrases were exchanged between the couple and the witnesses, thus bringing everyone into the service. These two methods are also traditional to most religious rites. Many couples in personal weddings have written their own joint or responsive readings; others have adapted readings from church books. This is a wide open area, since a couple may choose secular or religious readings to use as a joint or responsive reading. Here is one responsive reading that comes from a Presbyterian church in Oregon.

MINISTER: This couple comes together out of a community of friends and relatives. They ask our support as they together begin the adventure of married life. . . . We come today to join in marriage _____ and _____. It is our hope that their individual lives may together explore new dimensions of life.

COMMUNITY: We dedicate ourselves to the continuing task of helping them in all ways possible to build a deep and abiding love.

MINISTER: We ask for them the excitement of new discoveries and new creations, that their lives may be an adventure together wherever they may go.

COMMUNITY: We dedicate ourselves to the continuing task of helping them in all ways possible to live the most fully human life.

MINISTER: We know that love is not a state of being easily achieved. We ask that _____ and _____ find the courage and the patience to overcome any obstacles, to open a profound communication—the very cornerstone of all relationships of love.

COMMUNITY: We dedicate ourselves to the continuing task of helping them in all ways possible to meet the challenge of a marriage pledged to honest struggle, open words, and shared lives.

MINISTER: We recognize that love is not limited nor can it be contained. We ask that the unique expression of love that _____ and _____ feel for each other reach out beyond themselves—to their family and to the world in which they live.

COMMUNITY: We dedicate ourselves to the continuing task of helping them in all ways possible to let their love so shine that it touches all who know them; and may their lives be lived not only for themselves, but for all men.

For responsive or joint readings and for many of the other alternatives that encourage participation, it is essential to have enough copies of the words to pass out to the guests.

5. Community singing of either religious or secular songs is another time-honored way of involving the participants at a wedding. Here again, choices are numerous. What you have to do is choose appropriate songs, make copies of the words, and perhaps of the music, for everyone, then designate someone to begin the singing at the right time.

6. One of the most important aspects of participation is the act of *sharing*. Singing is a way of sharing; greeting people or having group readings are other ways of achieving the closeness people feel when an emotion is being shared. The reception feast is the usual time when food and drink are communally

shared; everyone joins the celebration simply by eating together. Like so many other parts of the wedding, this concept is ancient; shared joy and responsibility are fundamental to the laws of marriage.

In numerous personal weddings, couples are finding other ways to bring a sense of community sharing into the ceremony itself. Along with singing and reciting, couples and their guests are also sharing bread and wine as an informal communion. The couples walk around to each guest and offer bread and wine so all will partake in the wedding feast. In reviving this old tradition, couples have wanted to extend their bond to include everyone present, thus involving the guests with symbolic acts as well as spoken words. Jewish couples have always shared wine during the ceremony to represent love and the bonds of matrimony. Recently we have heard of many Jewish weddings where the guests also were included in this ritual. For most couples who share food and drink during the wedding, the aim is more symbolic than religious; they have gone back to primitive times to revive this custom.

Sharing food is a form of communion, but there are other ways of expressing togetherness, too. In several weddings, the bride and groom have gone around to the guests at a point in the ceremony, speaking with each briefly and giving a kiss, hug, or handshake. Instead of waiting for the receiving line at the reception, these couples have wanted the "communion" to take place during the ceremony.

7. Many couples are setting aside time during the service for their friends and relatives to share something verbally with the couple and with the other par-

ticipants. During this time, guests might rise and say something personal about the couple, read a poem or a passage, sing a song, or in some other way make a gift of this kind to those being married. In some weddings only five or ten minutes were devoted to this type of participation, but in others it has lasted over an hour.

Some couples inform their guests beforehand that there will be a period of time for their participation. Others simply make time at the end of the ceremony. In departing from the highly structured service, couples gain some surprise and spontaneity by asking their guests to say or read something in this way. Many people don't care to speak, but after two or three have spoken to the couple, others generally want to express their feelings, too. Many couples have said that the most dramatic and emotion-filled part of the ceremony was when the guests began to speak to them.

Such was the case at one wedding when, just after the exchange of marriage vows, the groom said, "We would like to have you, our good friends and relatives, share with everyone any thoughts or feelings you are having at this moment." There was a long silence at first, but people then did join in, and they stayed for twenty minutes, talking and laughing, letting out some of the emotions that had built up during the ceremony.

8. Many couples involve their friends and relatives in the ceremony in a more structured way by arranging beforehand the various roles each will play. For example, some couples ask the best man or maid of honor to read something. In a Rochester, New York, ceremony, a friend of the groom's rose from the congregation at a prearranged time and read a passage

from the Book of Ruth. In a California wedding, the best man and maid of honor each told a small story about the couple—how they had met, when they got engaged, and a few other personal things.

A popular alternative for structured participation is to have the bride's attendant read a poem, prayer, passage, or something else the bride has chosen or written, to the groom, and to have the groom's attendant do the same to the bride. To convey how this might work, and also to suggest how relaxed the planning of an alternative wedding may be, we include this letter written by a groom to his best man:

JEFF,
As part of the marriage service, you and Gail's matron of honor get to read something. So, here's something from me for you to read to Gail. This is from the writings of Walter Rinder.

> For me to love is to commit myself, freely and without reservation. I am sincerely interested in your happiness and well being. Whatever your needs are, I will try to fulfill them. If you are lonely and need me, I will talk. If you need the strength of human touch, I will touch you. If you need to be held, I will hold you.
> I will try to be constant with you so that you will understand the core of my personality and from that understanding you can gain strength and security that I am acting as me.
> I want to become a truly loving person. Knowing you has opened me to a new and different understanding of what a loving attitude and way of life can mean. It

it my hope that our lives together may be a continual renewal of our love for one another and for other people.

If you would like, you can preface the reading with some remarks of your own about us, or me, or whatever, like I did for you, although Gail's friend probably won't, I don't know. Call or write and let us know when to expect you, exactly, please. Thanks.

CHIP

9. Finally, here is an example of the standard community participation in the revised Episcopal Church service. Some other church denominations include this vow of the congregation, and, in essence, they are alike. The minister addresses the wedding party and guests: "Will you who witness these vows do all in your power to support and uphold this marriage in the years ahead?" The congregation answers: "We will."

POETRY AND OTHER READINGS

Poetry and other short readings evoke a special mood. Like music, readings can express thoughts and emotions that are out of the ordinary, that are beautiful and special to the wedding day. Each couple chooses one or more passages that are personal to them when they decide to read at their wedding, and usually the poem or passage is selected to convey an idea or create an atmosphere. We have found that most couples having personal weddings want to express their feelings of love, joy, or promise in a unique way. Those who like to write often create passages themselves. But the many who find it difficult to put their emotions into words turn to writers and poets for their readings.

Choosing readings is not difficult, if you give your-selves enough time to look. Many people have long-time favorites. If not, there are thousands of poems, books, stories, and essays where you can find the words that are fitting for you. The search can be enjoyable if it is not too rushed; many couples say that the proc-ess of choosing works to read at their wedding was a time of sharing ideas and thoughts about the shape and substance of the ceremony and the marriage itself. At the wedding, the passages or poems can be read by one or both of the couple, by the officiant, by a designated member of the wedding party, or by all the guests in unison. Many couples report that their readings very effectively involved all their guests, and that most peo-ple were pleased with the participation.

It would be impossible to repeat all of the beauti-ful and powerful passages that have been read at per-sonal weddings. Nor do we want to, because half the fun is for the couple to find them on their own. We offer several examples of works used at recent cere-monies to give you an idea of the type of work nu-merous couples have found fitting.

1. Two of the most popular readings used at al-ternative weddings are from *The Prophet* by Kahlil Gibran. First, passages from "On Love."

> Love gives naught but itself and takes
> naught but from itself.

Love possesses not nor would it be possessed;
For love is sufficient unto love.

When you love you should not say, "God is
in my heart," but rather, "I am in the
heart of God."

And think not you can direct the course
of love, for love, if it finds you worthy,
directs your course.

Love has no other desire but to fulfill itself.
But if you love and must needs have desires,
let these be your desires:
To melt and be like a running brook that
sings its melody to the night.
To know the pain of too much tenderness.
To be wounded by your own understanding
of love;
And bleed willingly and joyfully.
To wake at dawn with a winged heart and
give thanks for another day of loving;
To rest at the noon hour and meditate
love's ecstasy;
To return home at eventide with gratitude;
And then to sleep with a prayer for the
beloved in your heart and a song of
praise upon your lips.

The second passage—perhaps the most often used
—is titled "On Marriage."

You were born together, and together you shall be
    forevermore.
You shall be together when the white wings of death
    scatter your days.
Ay, you shall be together even in the silent memory
    of God.
But let there be spaces in your togetherness,
And let the winds of heaven dance between you.

Love one another, but make not a bond of love:
Let it rather be a moving sea between the shores of
    your souls.
Fill each other's cup but drink not from one cup.
Give one another of your bread but eat not from the
    same loaf.
Sing and dance together and be joyous, but let each
    one of you be alone,
Even as the strings of a lute are alone though they
    quiver with the same music.

Give your hearts, but not into each other's keeping.
For only the hand of Life can contain your hearts.
And stand together yet not too near together:
For the pillars of the temple stand apart,
And the oak tree and the cypress grow not in each
    other's shadow.

    2. Standing before his bride and the rabbi, one
groom read the following poem by Charles Marcan-
tonio (from the introduction to Clark Moustakas' book
Individuality and Encounter).

Let us communicate in the language of being
Touching, feeling, sensing
I have no need to define or classify you
Or "know about" you
My heart reveals in silence that you are beautiful
And that is good
I want to meet with you in a spirit beyond possession
A spirit that allows us to be what we must
With freedom to flow together or to be Alone
I want to transcend time and space
And affirm our ephemeral being
With the eternal value of Love.

3. The following passage was written by the
bride's daughter and read by the minister during the
ceremony.

Believing all men to be interrelated, dependent, and
one in humanity, the relationship of two people who
deeply care for one another provides an opportunity for
us all to share in the celebration of their love. We have
come together as one family united by this love, to witness Ellen and Tom's wedding vows—pledges made
sacred by their willingness to share, to give, and "to be"
through and with each other.

A marriage brings two individuals into a unique relationship with one another—one which grows and de-
velops as each continues to experience both himself and
others. Mature love is union under the condition of preserving one's integrity. Such love allows us to overcome
our sense of isolation and separateness yet permits us to

retain our identity as persons. In love the paradox occurs that two people become one and yet remain two.

4. Of modern poets, E. E. Cummings' poems are among those most often read at personal weddings. Unlike many contemporary poets, his work is often joyous and simple—and a celebration of love. We offer two of his poems that are representative of the many that have been chosen.

if everything happens that can't be done
(and anything's righter
than books
could plan)
the stupidest teacher will almost guess
(with a run
skip
around we go yes)
there's nothing as something as one

one hasn't a why or because or although
(and buds know better
than books
don't grow)
one's anything old being everything new
(with a what
which
around we come who)
one's everyanything so

so world is a leaf so tree is a bough
(and birds sing sweeter

than books
tell how)
so here is away and so your is a my
(with a down
up
around again fly)
forever was never till now

now i love you and you love me
(and books are shuter
than books
can be)
and deep in the high that does nothing but fall
(with a shout
each
around we go all)
there's somebody calling who's we

we're anything brighter than even the sun
(we're everything greater
than books
might mean)
we're everyanything more than believe
(with a spin
leap
alive we're alive)
we're wonderful one times one

This second poem by Cummings has been read by
the groom to the bride:

somewhere i have never travelled,gladly beyond
any experience,your eyes have their silence:
in your most frail gesture are things which enclose
        me,
or which i cannot touch because they are too near

your slightest look easily will unclose me
though i have closed myself as fingers,
you open always petal by petal myself as Spring opens
(touching skilfully,mysteriously)her first rose

or if your wish be to close me,i and
my life will shut very beautifully,suddenly,
as when the heart of this flower imagines
the snow carefully everywhere descending;

nothing which we are to perceive in this world equals
the power of your intense fragility:whose texture
compels me with the colour of its countries,
rendering death and forever with each breathing

(i do not know what it is about you that closes
and opens;only something in me understands
the voice of your eyes is deeper than all roses)
nobody,not even the rain,has such small hands

5. For some couples, weddings are political as well
as romantic events. One couple spoke to each other of
how they saw their marriage with respect to the peace
movement they both participated in actively. In another instance, a couple asked the officiant to read
poems by Ho Chi Minh.

Other couples who have respect for Eastern religions have added readings and vows from these religions to the Western wedding ceremony. This mixing of Eastern and Western thought, ritual, and literature is occurring more and more frequently in American weddings today.

6. Many other couples have tried to mix the old with the new. They have made up their own vows and prayers in some cases, but they also looked back into English, French, Greek, or Italian literature to find poems that balanced the ceremony and spoke through tradition. Couples have used selected works from Chaucer, Milton, Donne, Keats, Shelley, and, of course, Shakespeare in their weddings. Shakespeare's comic dramas are rich with quotes, particularly *A Midsummer Night's Dream*. A few of his sonnets are suitable for the wedding feast, too. The one most frequently cited is number 116.

> Let me not to the marriage of true minds
> Admit impediments. For love is not love
> Which alters when it alteration finds
> Or bends with the remover to remove.
> O, no! it is an ever-fixed mark
> That looks on tempests and is never shaken;
> It is the star to every wand'ring bark,
> Whose worth's unknown although his height be taken.
> Love's not Time's fool, though rosy lips and cheeks
> Within his bending sickle's compass come.
> Love alters not with his brief hours and weeks,
> But bears it out even to the edge of doom.
> > If this be error, and upon me proved,
> > I never writ, nor no man ever loved.

7. The Bible, of course, offers numerous passages which couples planning personal weddings build into their ceremonies. Before the 1960s, most churches were strict about the readings from the Bible considered acceptable at weddings. Since then, many major churches have revised and expanded the selections so that more choices are now available within the church structure. But for many couples, even the prescribed readings are not enough; so they have found other passages that better reflect their religious, and personal, feelings.

One favorite is from Ecclesiastes, and it can be said or sung:

> For everything there is a season,
> and a time for every matter under heaven:
> a time to be born, and a time to die;
> a time to plant, and a time to pluck up what is
>   planted;
> a time to kill, and a time to heal;
> a time to break down, and a time to build up;
> a time to weep, and a time to laugh;
> a time to mourn, and a time to dance;
> a time to cast away stones, and
> a time to gather stones together;
> a time to embrace, and
> a time to refrain from embracing;
> a time to seek, and a time to lose;
> a time to keep, and a time to cast away;
> a time to rend, and a time to sew;
> a time to keep silence, and a time to speak;
> a time to love, and a time to hate;
> a time for war, and a time for peace.

Others have used selections from the Song of Songs, the beautiful wedding in the Old Testament. The Psalms have been used in interesting ways, too, either spoken or set to music. Again, the selections are so numerous we do not have room for them.

In many Christian services the traditional selections from the Bible often include the passage from Genesis telling of woman's birth from man's rib. This passage, and the one from Ephesians (5:21–23) which declares "Wives, be subject to your husbands as to the Lord; for the man is the head of the woman," etc., are being read less and less. Women's rights and the idea of equality between the sexes are rendering these ancient prescripts obsolete. As a result many couples look for other passages that reflect the equality of men and women more faithfully and do not stress the role of dominant man and submissive woman.

Two short passages that are widely used reflect the love and devotion at the wedding. Both are from the First Corinthians (13:4–7 and 11–13).

Love is patient and kind; love is not jealous or boastful; it is not arrogant or rude. Love does not insist on its own way; it is not irritable or resentful; it does not rejoice at wrong, but rejoices in the right. Love bears all things, believes all things, hopes all things, endures all things. . . . So faith, hope, love abide; but the greatest of these is love.

When I was a child, I spoke like a child, I thought like a child, I reasoned like a child; when I became a man, I gave up childish ways. For now we see in a mirror dimly, but then face to face. Now I know in part;

then I shall understand fully, even as I have been fully
understood. So faith, hope, love abide, these three; but
the greatest of these is love.

8. Many couples today are also turning to the
words of theologians, humanists, and psychologists for
passages to use in their weddings. Selections from Carl
Rogers, R. D. Laing, Barry Stevens, Martin Buber, and
Paul Tillich have been used very often at weddings in
the past several years. The following passage by Hugh
Prather, from his book *Notes to Myself,* is indicative
of one type of reading being used at many personal
ceremonies.

Love unites the part with the whole.
Love unites me with the world and with
myself. My life work could well be love.
Love is the universe complete. Detachment
is the universe divided. Detachment
divides me from myself and from others. Love is
the vision that can see all as one and one
as all: "I and my father are one." Is
there but one reality and one truth? Love
shows me where all minds and essences unite.

How do I get love? I have it. I must
drop my definitions of love. Love is not
saying nice things to people or smiling or
doing good deeds. Love is love. Don't
strive for love, be it.

I love because I love.

9. A minister in Oregon uses his own poem to begin many weddings at which he officiates. The poem expresses the ever-forward movement of life which brings a couple together and one day will separate them.

The old log in the woods will never be a great tree
    again
- - - things never go back - - - yet lying there - - -
covered with moss - - - it is creating new life - - -
which in turn will be great and beautiful. . . .

The fish eats the insect - - - the bird the fish - - -
the mammal the bird - - - and - - - the insect the
mammal - - - as each—in a universal rhythm is
creating new life - - - for there is no life except
life which comes from life. . . .

Waters flow where daisies grew - - -
Trees grow where swans once swam. . . .

All things upon this earth are developing into new
things - - - from what is here must come what
is to be . . . there is no other material. . . .

This is the fulfillment of the promise of life - - -
nothing can be destroyed - - -
everything is being created. . . .

Just as couples are breaking away from the traditional ceremonies, officiants are also taking new directions in wedding services. Many priests, rabbis, and ministers throughout the country are rewriting nuptial rites, finding new alternatives, and helping couples better plan their own weddings. Many officiants are open to new ideas coming from the couple—they may read selections of your choosing or ones they have written themselves. The two final passages, both read by officiants in personal weddings, give still another idea of the values emerging in the clergy today. These passages, or ones like them, have become an integral part of the wedding ceremony for many brides and grooms. And not all readings are religious; many members of the clergy turn to secular writers for thoughts appropriate for the celebration. For example, this selection from *Inscape* by Ross Snyder:

Out of the wild exuberance of creation throughout millions of years, you two have appeared . . . each of you unique, distinctive, wonderously personal. You have chosen to journey together down this earth valley in the brief moment of time that is yours. From this day forward, you become a unit of life that will bring forth futures. You are both called into a new existence. The old things have passed away; a new heaven and a new earth is now your dwelling place. For the whole universe has come to each of you in the form of a particular person who has a unique love for you and is beloved by you.

This final passage—the well-known "Desiderata" by an unknown author—followed one particular wedding. The officiant spoke the words just before the recessional, adding at the end, "Go in peace."

Go placidly amid the noise and the haste, and remember what peace there may be in silence. As far as possible without surrender be on good terms with all persons. Speak your truth quietly and clearly; and listen to others . . . ; they too have their story. Be yourself. Especially do not feign affection. Neither be cynical about love; for in the face of all aridity and disenchantment, it is as perennial as the grass . . . nurture strength of spirit to shield you in sudden misfortune. But do not distress yourself with imaginings. Many fears are born of fatigue and loneliness. Beyond a wholesome discipline, be gentle with yourself. You are a child of the universe . . . the universe is unfolding as it should. Therefore, be at peace with God . . . in the noisy confusion of life, keep peace with your soul.

PRAYERS

Having the blessings of the spirits or gods has been of primary importance in every society on earth, probably for all of human history. Offering prayers for a couple at the wedding, therefore, is an ancient practice, originally used to invoke the benevolent spirits and to keep away the evil ones. If a union was "acceptable" to the Greater Powers, then the couple could be assured of some tranquility or prosperity. If the marriage was "unacceptable," then sorrow and misfortune were sure to follow. Thus, prayers for happiness, prosperity, many children, and a long life were central to the wedding ceremony; in some cultures, prayers alone made up the entire service.

The wedding, and prayers dedicated to it, are seen in a different light today. Few people believe that the prayers said at weddings will actually make a difference in the couple's married life. For the most part, prayers have become a formality, and in most traditional weddings one or two standard prayers are offered by the officiant or, in some churches, by the entire congregation. For many, these prayers have lost their meaning.

But not for everyone. Many couples who have planned personal wedding ceremonies have written their own prayers or found ones more suited to them than the traditional ones. Their prayers reflect more fully the hopes and values and the most cherished goals they seek. Most couples have one or two prayers in the ceremony, but some have used six or seven short prayers which involve the guests as well as the wedding party.

Certainly not all couples will want to include prayers in their services, but for those who do, the possibilities for writing one's own prayers are endless. The officiant will usually be helpful, either in finding alternative prayers or in writing new ones. Here are some examples of the type of prayers that couples and officiants have offered in recent years. Some are secular, some religious.

1. The following prayer was read by the community and the minister in unison in a Chicago wedding:

We ask for Karen and Neil a full life—a life rich in meaning, in purpose, in caring, and in joy. We ask not that they be "happy ever after," although we hope they will feel happy, often. We ask what is perhaps a more realistic goal, though by no means a simple one: that they may continually strive to do and be what their inner voices urge them on to attain. Not a static contentment with each other and with their world, but an ongoing process of exploring the fullness of their own and each other's personality; of helping and being helped by others; of working for the survival of our endangered planet.

But let us not ask for them that which we would not want for ourselves. Let us join with them, and play with them, and work with them, through many more years of friendship and of love.

2. One couple who planned their own wedding totally and did not have a usual officiant wrote this very short prayer to end the ceremony:

Bless, O Lord, this wedding, these people, and this day. Amen.

3. In the traditional Catholic wedding service, there is a time for "The Prayers of the Faithful," when certain prayers are offered by the priest; then, after each prayer, the congregation responds, "Lord, hear our prayer." This structure offers many possibilities for the personal wedding. For instance, the bride and groom could write their own prayers, expressing their hopes for their own lives, for their loved ones, and for the whole society. Members of the congregation could freely offer their own prayers for the couple or for others. After each prayer, said by the couple or other

participants, everyone would respond, "Lord, hear our prayer."

4. A couple in Detroit altered their traditional Christian service in many ways. One way was to add prayers from the Gospels that usually are not offered during the wedding ceremony. This is just one example; it was recited by the whole congregation:

Peace I bequeath to you, my own peace I give you,
a peace the world cannot give, this is my gift to you.
Do not let your hearts be troubled or afraid.
You heard me say:
I am going away, and shall return.

(John 14:27–28)

This was followed by other selections from the Gospels and concluded with the traditional Lord's prayer. Their ceremony was very religious; yet it differed greatly from the normal service because this couple added many elements—new prayers, secular readings, new music, and so on. They kept the traditional structure, but expanded it to meet their desires.

5. Interfaith marriages are far more frequent now than they have been in recent years. When the bride is of one faith and the groom is of another, or one of the two is of no faith, prayers can be combined or, as many have done, denominational prayers can be eliminated and replaced by more general ones. We have recently seen a more frequent blending of Eastern prayers with the traditional Judeo-Christian ones, too. Couples who combine elements from many religions say they are striving to make a ritual that is not defined

or confined by one narrow definition. Thus, one couple in the Midwest took prayers from the Bible, the Koran, and the Hindu sacred book, the Upanishads.

The following prayer was written, and read aloud, by a couple at their wedding. The bride was Jewish and the groom Catholic. Neither wanted to renounce their religion of birth, although neither practiced that faith fully at the time of their wedding. *Belief* meant a great deal to them, but not in the confines of their original faiths.

Blessed be God, Creator of the earth and all its fruits. We praise you for this day and all the days that have brought us to it and all the days that will flow from it.

We thank you for our families. You have carved us from the lives of many nations, and made our blood vibrate with the heritage of many peoples. You have strengthened us through the journeys and hardships of our grandparents, taught us love and understanding through our parents, and in our brothers and sisters shown us the joy of sharing life.

Glory to you, Lord, for bringing us together. You have given us this day to celebrate our love. Before today, we each had known joy, felt sorrow, seen triumph, endured struggle, lived with our strengths and weaknesses. These elements shaped our lives. In your wisdom, they somehow also shaped the long winding road that brought us to each other. Today, our roads unite. Today we celebrate our love. Surely, our lives will see more joy and more sorrow, but now we will accept them as one. God, our help in ages past, be our strength in years to come.

We ask you, Lord, to hear us. May the joining of our lives be fruitful for us and all we meet. May our love be an instrument of peace, our home a Temple of joy, our unity a reminder that all men are brothers. May our children remember us for making life wonderful. May they stand in awe of you, the God of us all.

6. At an outdoor wedding in the mountains of Colorado, the couple recited a prayer they had written to nature. For them, religion was nature itself, and their prayer asked for the help of all people to keep nature protected and beautiful. During the prayer, which was quite long and made up most of the ceremony, the couple requested that their guests participate by adding to the invocation.

7. Finally, we include two prayers used by a minister from the West in ceremonies he has helped write and design. The first short prayer follows the "Call to Celebration" by the officiant:

God, for the joy of this occasion we thank you; for the meaning of this wedding day we thank you; for this important moment in an evergrowing relationship we thank you; for your presence here and now and for your presence at all times we thank you. In Christ's name, Amen.

The second prayer can be placed anywhere in the ceremony.

Almighty God: We ask that the promise and hope of this marriage be fulfilled.

May the happiness and intimacy of this time be recalled many times.

May this marriage be a course of independent strength and will; a center and respite from endless turning; a still reflection of connected lives; a pleasant recollection of the past; and a ribbon of bright love through the future.

May this couple's anger at themselves and the world be honest and lively; may silence and despair never separate them; may they always return to each other.

May their lives lie quiet beneath the flow of change.

May their friends welcome them again in other times and other seasons.

We ask this in the name of the Creator who is the ground of all things. Amen.

VOWS, CONTRACTS, AND COMMITMENTS

One of the most commonly accepted myths about the wedding ceremony is that it must conform to a prescribed church service in order to be valid. Actually, the legality of a marriage is determined by state law, not church customs. Each church sets its own standards for its members—and a wedding that is legally sound may not be recognized by a particular church denomination because it did not conform to that church's religious standards. On the whole, church standards have been more strict than those of the State.

However, most major churches have liberalized their wedding services in the past ten years—in part because so many couples wanted to change the traditional patterns. Many of the old restrictions have been replaced by a more flexible set of doctrines in which the church prescribes not one, but several sanctioned alternatives at different points in the ceremony. Yet a growing number of clergy would like to go even further and are committed to the idea of the "open ceremony," or what we are calling here the personal wedding. Thus, even with the newly revised services, the question of what constitutes a true "religious wedding" is still an open one for thousands of priests, rabbis, and ministers.

Actually, wedding vows can take any form the couple wants and still be legal—as long as the bride and groom have purchased a marriage license, have had a blood test if required by the state where the wedding will take place, have official recognition of the marriage (by an officiant licensed by the state), and have the marriage certificate signed by two witnesses affirming that the wedding took place. Legally, these are the only requirements. If a couple chose to be married in utter silence, and the above steps were taken, their marriage would be valid.

The confusion about the legality of some personal weddings comes about mainly because most people *assume* a couple must be married with the words of a church service in order for the wedding to be "real." Again, the assumption is incorrect; it comes from being so accustomed to one form of marriage that anything which deviates from the norm seems wrong. In fact, personal weddings are just as valid as those celebrated with a High Mass. There is no set of words which, if said, instantly marry a couple. Vows repeated in church services are drawn up and approved by each church hierarchy; the vows differ from church to church. The reason most Christian weddings sound alike is because they all have the same common sources: the Bible, Roman and English civil and Canon law, and the various folk traditions that are deeply rooted in the marriage heritage.

But even though the "accepted" vows are not mandatory, for well over two thousand years couples have used vows of one kind or another in weddings. Why? Aside from the official reasons, vows serve an enormously important role in a marriage: they publicly affirm the intentions of the couple to love, trust, and honor. For most people, the promises and commitments made on the wedding day in the form of vows are the central core of the marriage rite. Weddings join two people legally, but the vows each partner makes to the other are what join them emotionally. It is these intentions which they declare that form the real bond between them.

Many of the couples we interviewed said they began thinking about alternatives to the traditional wedding when they discussed the importance of the vows. They simply did not want to use the same words repeated by millions of other couples. They wanted to express more fully the nature of their own, particular commitments in marriage. Others questioned specific aspects of the traditional vows. "Love, honor and obey," "till death us do part," and "as long as we both shall live" are the objectionable phrases cited most often.

Once the couples began reexamining the vows,

they found themselves asking, "What does this marriage mean to *me*, to *us?*" Soon they began to change or reinterpret numerous other elements in the ceremony. One man summed up his feelings about the wedding this way: "If we can't get married on our own terms, with our own ideas of what we want our lives together to be like, then why bother at all? We didn't want to recite some old church vows. We wanted our own thoughts, ones we were committed to live with." This is what most people seem to have in mind when they depart from the old to make new alternatives.

Like most other elements in personal weddings, the vows we have seen and heard vary greatly. Some are short and simple, some very long. Many recent weddings have included the reading of a contract between husband and wife—not really formal documents, but issues and attitudes the couples want to make public. These "contracts" cover a large range of topics, from child care to financial matters. In all cases, the importance of the vows to the couples was not just to become "legally married" by a set formula. The real point was that each couple set their own standards and made promises they believed were realistic for themselves.

The following examples of vows and contracts have come from recent weddings.

1. "I promise to love, to honor, and to cherish you —to live with you as your (husband) (wife)—so long as we both shall love."

2. "I promise to be with you and for you; to share

my life, my feelings, my hopes, and my experiences with you; to respect your individuality; and to love you. I give you this ring as a symbol of my promise."

3. Minister: Will you now affirm your trust and love for each other?

Bride and Groom in unison: I draw you unto my very being to share with you life's sorrows and joys. I promise to respect you and be respected by you; to forgive you and be forgiven by you; to instill hope in you and be given hope by you. I promise to accept the mystery of your unique selfness and to love you as Thou. Through these acts of teaching and learning, we grow toward each other.

4. In a wedding in New York City, the Ethical Culture leader who officiated asked the couple to write their own vows. This is what they read to each other in the ceremony:

BRIDE: My dear Peter, I stand secure within the circle of your love, to which I add my love for you. May we ever stand thus, though our circles expand to include others, close within the ring of strength and faith our love has formed.

GROOM: Lynn, dearest, the decision we make here is the first immutable one of our lives. We distinctly, with our full understanding, bind each other's life to our own. It is not easy to venture onto this road of accepting the responsibility of, and sharing in, the joys of your life, but I do so truly and faithfully pledge.

5. In a religious ceremony in the Midwest, the bride and groom planned and wrote the entire service. They borrowed some elements from the traditional service, but they also added many new and personal readings, including their vows. A member of the wedding party served as a "Commentator," introducing new parts and directing the guests when to join in the readings. Here is a section of the ceremony.

COMMENTATOR: Marriage is not a sacrament which is performed by priest or deacon. It is given by the bride and groom to each other—they administer the sacrament one to another. Yet it is also a gift given in the name of the faithful community to all mankind, a renewal, through these two, of the covenant between man and God.

OFFICIANT: In the name of this holy assembly, I ask you _____, do you take _____ as your lawful wife, according to the rite of God's People, the Church?

GROOM: I do.

OFFICIANT: In the name of this holy assembly, I ask you _____, do you take _____ as your lawful husband, according to the rite of God's People, the Church?

BRIDE: I do.

ALL PRESENT:

"You dare your Yes—and experience
a meaning.
You repeat your Yes—and all things
acquire a meaning.
When everything has a meaning, how
can you live anything but a Yes."
(Dag Hammarskjold, *Markings*)

Exchange of Vows. First the groom and then the bride said:

I, _____, promise you, _____, to be your (husband) (wife) forever. As your (husband) (wife) I promise to continue to love you and to spread our love to others, to seek peace in and with you, for ourselves, for our children, and for our suffering universe, and to find joy in and with you and through the laughter of all that is. And I promise to be responsible for you forever, because I love you.

ALL:

Lord, make them an instrument of your peace.
Where there is hatred, let them bring love.
Where there is injury, pardon. Where there is doubt, faith.
Where there is despair, hope. Where there is darkness, light.
Where there is sadness, joy. Grant that they may not so much seek to be consoled as to console, to be understood as to understand, to be loved as to love.

The exchange of rings followed. The groom read a section from the Book of Proverbs and the bride read Psalm 112 "as a symbol of my love for you and my hope in you." Then everyone again read this short passage from Hammarskjold's *Markings*:

Every deed and every relationship is surrounded by an atmosphere of silence.

Friendship needs no words—it is solitude
delivered from the anguish of loneliness.

6. Instead of the traditional "giving away" of the daughter by her father, many couples include both parents in the vows in new ways. This is one example.

RABBI: Norman, Carla has indicated she wants to be your wife. Now I ask will you give yourself to her? Will you try always to share completely with her in your life together? Will you try always to be open and honest in your relationship? Will you try always to give her all comfort and support and strength?

GROOM: I will.

RABBI: Carla, Norman has indicated he wants to be your husband. Now I ask will you give yourself to him? Will you try always to share completely with him in your life together? Will you try always to be open and honest in your relationship? Will you try always to give him all comfort and support and strength?

BRIDE: I will.

RABBI: In marriage, two people leave established families and begin a new life together. (To the parents, by name) ————, ————, ————, ————, will you try, with the greatest love and wisdom you can command, to support this new couple and to help them in every way?

PARENTS: We will.

GROOM: I, Norman, take you, Carla, to be my wife; and I promise, in the midst of our families and friends (and God) to stand beside and with you always; in times of celebration and times of sadness; in times of

pleasure and times of anger; in times of pain and times
of health; I will live with you and love you as long as
we are one, as long as we both shall live (love).

BRIDE: I, Carla, take you, Norman, to be my husband;
and I promise, in the midst of our families and friends
(and God) to stand beside and with you always; in
times of celebration and times of sadness; in times of
pleasure and times of anger; in times of pain and times
of health; I will live with you and love you as long as
we are one, as long as we both shall live (love).

7. Until recently, it has generally been assumed
that a man would look for a woman to marry who
shared his religious beliefs. Because interfaith marriages are increasing, personal wedding services are a
necessity for many couples. Neither bride nor groom
wants to be forced to follow the traditional rites of the
other's religion, so compromises and combinations of
services often result.

In some cases, couples have said that they discarded all aspects of their separate religious services
and started from scratch to write their own. In this way
they avoided any feelings of resentment between them.

Others turned to different solutions. One couple
who believed in ecumenism found a priest, a minister,
and a rabbi to officiate together at their wedding. Each
officiant added a portion of a traditional service to the
wedding, and all the elements fit together very well.

In another "mixed" wedding, the priest read a passage of the nuptial communion in Hebrew. It was discovered at the rehearsal that the Catholic words were
almost identical to the Hebrew blessing, and the cou-

ple wanted as much combination of the traditional services as possible.

Many couples who have had to face the problem of differing beliefs have said it took a while to talk out the issues and decide on the alternatives. But the majority were very satisfied with the results of their efforts to create a new wedding rite for themselves. One woman wrote, "If Jim and I had both been Jewish (I am, he's a Protestant), we probably would have settled for the usual temple service and not thought much about it. As it was, we worked out a plan for our ceremony that was still religious, but took advantage of the best parts of the two services. It took a lot of work, but it was fun—we really got together on it. And I know the wedding was more special to us because we'd worked it out ourselves. In many ways, it was the *process* that made the wedding so good." Jan and Ed, whose wedding was described in the first chapter, also were of different faiths. Three years later, they remember their wedding as being one of the most beautiful days in their lives. Ed writes: "There is a much closer identity with the marriage ceremony than I would expect you would find with other people, simply because we created it, and designed it to reflect what we were about. We're still about the same basic things."

8. Not only is the participation of two or more officiants a growing practice, but multiple marriages by one officiant are also becoming more common and popular, especially among young people. The double marriage has a long tradition, and in the past ten years the idea has been stretched to include five, ten, and

even up to seventy-five couples being married at one time.

Multiple couples wanting to get married have found officiants who will marry them *en masse*. In one instance seven couples, all friends beforehand, got together and wrote up a ceremony that lasted about twenty-five minutes. Each couple chose a poem or reading, and the vows were arrived at by the whole group by selecting elements from different Christian and Buddhist texts. When everyone had agreed on how the vows should read, they chose a date and were married together in Central Park in New York City. A part of their vows declared that they were dedicated to each person equally; each had a partner and legal husband or wife, but helping the whole "community" and each individual member was also an important promise.

The vow to stay close and be of aid to every person seems to be a common theme in most multiple marriages. Usually there is a cause or a movement that holds all the couples together, and their vows reflect that sense of community purpose. This was the case in the huge wedding in California in the summer of 1972 at the Synanon Ranch, a center for former drug addicts. In that ceremony, the Reverend Mason Harvey officiated at the union of seventy-five Synanon couples. Each couple, the officiant, and the more than two thousand guests were dressed in frontier garb reminiscent of a century ago. Part of the reason for the size of the group was their shared commitment to stay "clean," away from all drugs. The support of the group —and the uniqueness of the situation—was thought to help all members achieve the goal of rehabilitation.

9. Marriages within the Quaker community have always been simple, religious affairs. In recent years, the Quaker-style ceremony has provided an example for hundreds of couples who were searching for alternatives from the usual church service. While couples who are not members of the Religious Society of Friends cannot have an authentic Quaker wedding, its format has been inspirational to many non-Quakers.

In the Quaker ceremony, the couple enters the traditional Meeting, the gathering of community and friends, and goes to the front of the room. The bride's father does not give her away, nor is there an officiant to pronounce them "married." The Quakers believe that only God can make that kind of union. The couple hold hands and make a simple promise, or vow. The standard one is: "In the presence of God and these our friends, I take thee _____ to be my (wife) (husband), promising with Divine assistance to be unto thee a loving and faithful (husband) (wife) so long as we both shall live."

Then the couple signs the marriage certificate, and all those present also sign. Sometimes prayers are offered, and someone may make a brief statement; but the wedding itself is the repeating of vows by the couple in the presence of the group.

Many non-Quaker couples have used this idea for their personal weddings. The vows differ, and perhaps more elements have been added, but the result has been a sincere and beautiful ceremony.

Contracts

Marriage "contracts" are usually designed to take the vows one step further in definition. The contract has emerged from the growing trend among couples having personal weddings to define their goals and responsibilities clearly for each other, before the marriage takes place.

Each couple that writes a contract for their marriage has different ends in mind; but there is one important aspect in common. These couples are not blindly accepting the roles and values their culture has always assumed for them. In making a contract, the couple is trying to explain and clarify how their marriage can and will be run. They are entering marriage with a well-thought-out idea of what problems they are likely to encounter. And by trying to deal with these areas before the big problems arise, they are usually helping to minimize the trouble.

The desire for equality and fairness often prompts couples to write a contract. Many women want more help with domestic chores, or they do not assume that domestic chores are primarily their responsibility in the first place. Similarly, many men want it made clear that they need not bear the sole or even main burden of the financial responsibilities.

The old stereotypes of men and women are certainly breaking down today, but there is also a strong tradition, at least twenty-five hundred years old, of dominant-male-breadwinner and submissive-female-homemaker to overcome. And it isn't easy. In writing contracts, couples hope to establish goals and standards for their lives so that both partners can grow as individuals and still enjoy their life together.

Marriage contracts take many different forms. Some are actually legal documents, which may or may not be read at the wedding service. Some couples, for example, want to be sure that, in case of divorce, principles of equality will govern the settlement rather than the legal norm which at least on paper tends to favor women, an ironic benefit of a traditionally inferior role.

As one woman explained the importance of a contract, "It wasn't that we doubted our love or didn't plan on making the marriage work, hopefully, forever. But we wanted to be realistic, too. Let's face it—almost all couples figure their marriage will last forever; but the statistics show that a good percentage of them don't. People may love each other deeply when they get married, but ten years later get involved in incredibly bitter disputes over a divorce settlement. Well, we just wanted to make sure that whatever happened, we wouldn't end up like so many other couples we've seen —such pain, such prolonged legal misery. It took us about an hour to write our contract and then a short time with our lawyer. That's all. And it's sure nice to know we'll never have to worry about making a divorce even harder by having us and our lawyers fighting with each other for months on end. Naturally, we're optimistic about the success of our marriage. But then, you don't plan on getting into an accident, but you buy auto insurance anyway."

What this couple contracted was three simple agreements: (1) If one party wants a divorce, for any reason, the second party may ask for a six-month waiting period, after which he/she must grant the divorce if the first party still wants it. (2) In the event of divorce, no alimony will be paid by either party. (3) In the event of divorce, all jointly owned property will be divided equally between both parties. This last point was based upon a previous understanding the couple had arrived at about how to handle their finances. They had agreed to each keep their separate capital with which they entered the marriage; to pool all their annual income into a joint fund; and whenever the joint fund rose above a certain amount, the extra would be divided equally between them and go back into their separate capital. In that way they assured independence to both. Financially, however, they made their married life a joint project, each benefiting from the other's gains. They believed that both partners, whatever type of work they did—whether money-making, child care, or whatever—were supporting the partnership and were entitled to share equally in the "profits."

Most of the documents called "contracts" have been "agreements" between the bride and groom, not legally drawn papers. Some are simply a list of things the couple know they must work on in order to live together more easily. Others are very detailed, almost legalistic documents that spell out each partner's responsibilities. Without going into too much detail here, we want to offer some of the issues found most often in contracts we've seen.

1. Names. The woman's decision to keep her own name. Hyphenated names, that is, a combination of the bride's and groom's last names. Selection of a new name for both partners.

2. Finances. Who is expected to earn how much? What part of the bills will each pay? Separate or joint checking accounts? How much savings each month? If the woman stays home to take care of children, how will she be compensated? If the husband wants to take time off and work on a project that may not earn a regular income, how can this be worked out? If divorce comes, will there be alimony? Child support? Etc.

3. Child care. How can the couple share the responsibility for raising and taking care of children? Who does what tasks? (Some couples have arrived at very complete schedules for taking care of children; they are often, but not always, half-and-half propositions.) What will the children's responsibilities be? How can the couple have some independent time, apart from their children? Etc.

4. Birth control. What are the couple's preferences here? Which methods do they regard as the safest? Which are most and least physically comfortable? Whose responsibility is it? Many couples work out arrangements making birth control a shared responsibility. Some couples agree that the wife will take the major responsibility for the first part of the marriage, but that later on—once they have had as many children as they want and feel fairly certain that neither will want any more—the husband will have a vasectomy. In one instance we know of, the couple decided that the wife would use a diaphragm half the

time, the husband a condom the other half. But no matter how each couple solves this issue, most people have said it was a difficult area to agree on instantly; it was often one that had to be discussed over a period of time.

5. Household jobs. Who does the cooking? The dishes? The laundry? The floors? Again, each couple has different circumstances, but the whole purpose in writing a contract is to make certain that fairness is maintained and that the couple does not automatically slip into the "usual" roles. By sharing the domestic jobs, and carefully describing who shall do what at a given time, many couples have found that restrictive definitions of their roles have not developed.

The National Organization for Women (NOW) has published a list of goals for revising marriage, divorce, and family laws. Many of these goals are the same issues that couples focus upon in their marriage contracts:

> . . . To equalize the rights of men and women to own property, establish domicile, maintain individual identity and economic independence; to equalize their obligations toward each other and toward the care and custody of children; to support a dependent spouse through a period of economic readjustment upon termination of a marriage; and to promote marriage as an equal partnership in all its aspects.

One reason that many couples have written private, rather than legally binding, marriage contracts is that they have found they have had to change and reinterpret many agreements as they went on in their married life. The important thing, most people have said, is that they spent the time *beforehand* to try to figure out what their problems might be after the euphoria of the honeymoon was over. In the process of talking out their questions, they dealt with many problems and issues they didn't even know were there. Again, it is the process, not the plan itself, that made the difference. There is no one correct form for a marriage contract. The issues and answers will vary greatly from couple to couple. But if both partners enter the bargain with independence and integrity accompanying their love, then whatever contract they agree on will probably be a viable one for them.

We should mention that not all contracts deal with the daily workings of the marriage. Many couples who read their contracts at their weddings have more general ideals in mind. They figure they can work out the nitty-gritty details alone, but they want to publicize the intent of equality and mutuality at their ceremony. Like the promises made in the wedding vows, these more general contracts are statements of love and trust. They are the guidelines for making the marriage honest, lively, and continually new.

The following "contract" was included with a Michigan couple's invitation, and later read aloud during the wedding ceremony.

Our Commitment

We seek to continue a stable relationship between two loving, affectionate people oriented toward sharing their growing lives. Neither of us wants to impose our own way of being on the other. In order to create a nurturant environment for our continued growth, together and as individuals, we must clarify some specific issues.

We each come to this relationship with certain primary needs, which if met on a continuing basis outside our relationship will threaten and weaken our bonds. We see these primary needs as being the basics of caring and sharing; the underlying elements in love and affection, empathy, encouragement, commitment, and celebration. It is these basics that help us to be supportive when we are down, and to express joy with and for each other.

It would be impossible for us to attain our ideal if we did not build individual freedom into our union. At the acknowledged risk of separation we must be true to ourselves, as we are now, and as we come to be. We must continue to explore and expand as persons, in order to grow as mates. Without the stimulation and security of friends, education, and creative leisure pursuits, we would stagnate together. Growth can only occur if we seek these opportunities together, as well as apart.

In all relationships there are decisions to be made, and responsibilities to be borne. Neither of us is willing to confer ultimate power on the other. We do, however, recognize natural authority. Therefore, while most decisions will be made jointly, by consensus and compromise, there will be times when one of us is better suited to making a decision and this will be recognized. Similarly responsibilities involving finance, job, and household will be shared. We must be flexible enough to allow for our aptitudes, our background differences, and the variance in our incomes. On the other hand we must avoid stereo-typing and rigid sex role casting. We seek a blend of the companionate and shared role patterns of relating.

In all things we expect and demand honesty and fair fighting. We recognize that neither of us can meet all of the other's needs. While we do not require exclusivity, outside involvements must be clearly communicated to our partner. Those involvements not mutually shared must also serve as a cue to understanding, reevaluating, and perhaps reworking our commitment. In the future we may seek a broader based shared relationship, but for now we seek a firm understanding and commitment for the two of us. Either of us at any time may request a review of this contract of commitment.

Promising lifetime permanence of relationship would be contradictory and self-defeating. We do expect our union to continue as long as it is fulfilling for both of us. In this kind of open ended contract, we build in the need and desire to assess our position and the joyous opportunity of recommitting ourselves every year, every month, every day. A major decision point will come if one or both of us begins to want children. Should we separate in our lifetimes neither of us will expect nor accept financial support from the other.

We intend to enjoy our time of life together. In this spirit we formalize our commitment to each other and before you. We continue with new fervor, a stable relationship between two loving affectionate people, oriented toward sharing their growing lives.

We marry, 7 October 1972.

Vows and contracts, as well as the giving of rings

as symbols of the union, are the central part of most couples' weddings. The joy—and the fear—of giving, of receiving, publicly, another person's love and commitment, is what all weddings are about. Promises are made, prayers offered, declarations proclaimed. People come together to witness and celebrate, to offer their support and love for the bride and groom. It is a feast of the human spirit, a tribute to the act of living.

FINAL WORD AND RECESSIONAL

Many personal weddings end with a Final Word —a prayer, a short comment by the officiant or a member of the wedding party, or a statement by the bride or groom. Sometimes it is simply "Thank you all for coming." Sometimes couples want to express more.

1. In a Texas wedding, just before the bride and groom left the church, all the guests stood and recited a prayer for the couple. Actually, the best man had passed out copies of the prayer before the ceremony, and the couple did not know about it. The groom said later, "We didn't know what was happening at first, but after we realized that about one hundred people were saying a prayer for us, for our future, we just stood there smiling and loving every one of them. It was a beautiful ending."

2. A minister in Oregon often ends weddings at which he officiates with this traditional benediction:

The Lord bless you and keep you, the Lord make his face to shine upon you, and be gracious

unto you; the Lord lift up his countenance
upon you, and give you peace. Amen.

3. At the end of one wedding, the groom read
this statement, which the bride and he had written.
An alternative would have been to have each read one
paragraph.

We wish to extend to you our warmest gratitude for
coming to share this moment with us. Since it is we who,
this day, performed the sacrament together, it is we who,
appropriately, have created this liturgy together. We
thank you for participating fully in the celebration, for
it is you who together witness and so seal the reality of
this event.

The interlocking circles on the wedding invitations
represent the coming-together of two persons, who become one through love, yet through love become as well
more fully themselves. The wedding rings also form a
band of interlocking circles, to indicate the sharing of
our love with others whom we have known and will
know. For it is the love that family and friends have
given us in the past which makes possible the present
union. And it is this love, given each of us by you today
united, which will ripple forth in ever-widening circles
to form new bonds and new unions in a joy-filled future.
Again, thank you all!

After everything is said and done, the couple must,
somehow, leave the site of the ceremony. In most traditional weddings, the recessional is formal; first the
bride and groom walk up the aisle, next the wedding

party, then the parents of the couple, and finally the guests.

In personal weddings, other methods of departure are sometimes used. Couples who have arrived in some unusual way often use the same method to leave— horses, buckboards, canoes, etc. Sometimes a special song is played, or the couple may literally dance away from the altar. To conclude this section on the ceremony, we offer a few examples of recent recessionals.

1. In a church where the ancient custom of throwing rice was prohibited, two thousand butterflies were released, in the church, at the end of the ceremony.

In another wedding, rose petals were strewn along the aisle, out the door, and up to the door of the car that took the couple away.

2. One couple in California played Janis Joplin's "Get It While You Can" as they left the home in which the wedding took place. They left smiling.

3. After one small personal ceremony, the couple went to the guests and asked that everyone hold hands as they departed from the field where the wedding had taken place. The whole line of people, led by the bride and groom, walked hand in hand across the field to the site of the reception.

4. A couple who were married on a mountain top in France in winter skied down the slopes to a chalet. Apparently this was the only means of transportation, so the guests had to follow suit.

5. Finally, in a simple departure from the formal recessional, one couple, at the end of their wedding,

walked out of the church arm-in-arm with both sets of parents.

Like all other aspects of the personal ceremony, the recessional is one more expression of the couples' values, their tastes, and, often, their sense of drama. A wedding which is otherwise carefully planned and lovingly executed can end disappointingly if the final words and recessional are not in keeping with the rest of the ceremony; or if the ending is not clearly identifiable for the guests. Although you may feel it to be, your wedding is not over when you become wife and husband. The final words and recessional are an integral part of the ceremony and deserve their due amount of time and attention in your planning.

THE RECEPTION

The wedding reception is as old as the wedding itself. The "reception" was originally the celebration that *received* the bride and groom into the community. Their new status as full members of the group was a very important event. The reception was—and still remains—the time for the couple and the guests to eat and drink together and, by this sharing, to symbolically make a bond for the future.

Wedding receptions have long been festive gatherings, often including an entire community, where the usual social constraints and laws were suspended and the spirit of joy and festival reigned. It was the time to "be one" with the new couple, to join in their happiness, wish them well, sing and dance, and be with friends and loved ones.

This idea of the wedding feast has not changed for thousands of years. It still holds firm today. And in this regard, there is little difference between the reception for a traditional wedding and one for a personal wedding. In spirit, they are similar.

The marriage of two people is a unique event, especially when old traditions are reevaluated and altered to fit the couple's life. But beyond a certain point, all parties, receptions, or other feasts are similar. People who gather to celebrate and enjoy themselves tend to do so in similar ways.

Yet, even though "a party is a party," and the reception for one wedding may seem very much like another, there can be some differences. The majority of those people we spoke with who have had personal weddings say they wanted their receptions to be more informal, less expensive, and more original than the receptions they had been to in the past. Most of them deliberately tried to change the focus from surfeit to simplicity, thereby changing the focus from the *party* to the *people*.

One young woman told us, "We tried to make our reception seem like a natural extension of the ceremony. Our wedding was pretty loose, and so was the party. We didn't want frills and tons of exotic foods. We just wanted to be with our friends and have a good time with them." Another woman who had a very informal reception said, "I had stood in too many formal receiving lines when I was a bridesmaid at my friends' weddings. I got to hate the artificial pomp of it all.

Everyone seemed like they were walking around in glass shoes, so stuffy, you know. I think the setting of those club receptions makes people feel uptight, not relaxed."

The most visible difference between traditional and personal receptions seems to be informality, an informality that covers many areas. Receiving lines are often omitted. Caterers are used less and less. Friends help with food preparation and clean-up. Huge, tiered wedding cakes are often replaced by homebaked cakes. Professional musicians are replaced by tapes and records. Dress is more informal and varied.

But again, these changes are only surface ones. Behind the growing change in receptions is a clear shift in values. Many couples who could afford a lavish, catered affair have chosen not to go that route because they saw it as a real waste of money. Some viewed the ornate reception as embarrassing. Others simply did not like the "sameness" of all the catered receptions and wanted, instead, to celebrate in a more informal, down-to-earth way. A recently married man put it this way. "Sure, we could have had a huge reception, piled to the ceiling with food and booze, that would have cost thousands of dollars. My wife's father said, 'Anything you want.' But we really didn't want what he expected. We didn't want our wedding to be remembered for the giant reception where everyone could feel like an ancient Roman. We wanted people to remember the *wedding*, which we had taken such time to plan, not how stuffed they got afterward. So instead of having it at his club, we held the reception in his backyard and catered only sandwiches and hors d'oeuvres. I think he was a little disappointed he couldn't give us a big bash, but everyone had a good time—and he saved himself a small fortune."

Several couples told us they had planned and carried out their own receptions because they thought it would reflect their wedding far better than something organized by someone else who didn't know them. One person said, "I can't understand how thousands of couples each year feel that, if they select the menu from a caterer, the reception is unique. For me, after attending many weddings, catered receptions are as alike as McDonald's hamburgers."

Catered or uncatered, handling food for a reception is the biggest problem. We have seen many ways that people have solved the problem imaginatively. No matter what the site of the reception, any couple can find many alternatives for feeding the guests. A couple in California had their wedding and reception on a large private boat. After the ceremony, a meal of different kinds of seafood was served, along with champagne and wine. There was no hot food. Most of the guests were in bathing suits, and the reception lasted for hours as people talked, ate, and swam. At nightfall the boat returned to dock and everyone went their way.

One of the most popular ways of handling food in recent years has been to ask guests to help out by donating a favorite dish for the party. Most guests bring one of their own specialties, so the result is a table spread with a wide variety of interesting, tasty foods. Of the many people we spoke to who had done their reception in this way, none said that any of their guests were offended by the practice. One woman recounted this story: "I was a little worried that some of my mother's friends would think I was crazy when I called to ask them to bring a favorite food for the reception. But what happened at the party was great. All those who cooked tried to make their nicest, fanciest recipe, and they were so happy when someone would compliment them on it. The reception cost us very little, and the food was fantastic. And all the cooks got a little ego boost, too."

A variation of this was seen in a Wisconsin wedding and reception held in a large public park and beach on the shores of Lake Superior. Guests were asked to bring picnic lunches. All the food—sandwiches, salads, cold chicken, etc.—was spread on a large table and everyone could pick what they wanted. The bride's parents took care of soft drinks, wine, and beer. During the reception, people played volleyball, swam, canoed, or sailed. The reception lasted about seven hours—and no one went home hungry.

Many couples are choosing to treat their receptions as a simple gathering of friends, making no pretense about having a traditional reception. A young couple going to college in Maine decided to get married during the school term. They invited about fifteen close friends. Because they had very little money, and no help from their parents, they held the wedding and reception in the home of a teacher-friend. The food consisted of pizza, beer, and a few dips for chips. Although it was small and inexpensive, both the bride and groom said they preferred that kind of party to a more formal one. In fact, the reason they got married when and where they did was to avoid a huge wedding and reception that the bride's mother had wanted and could not be talked out of. We have heard of receptions that were even simpler than this—for example, serving Hawaiian Punch and wedding cake in the church basement following the ceremony. The old assumption for many couples was that you *had to* have a big reception. Many couples today seem to be assuming the opposite—that you don't have to have any reception if you don't want to. Thus, the type of party they eventually decide on is one that they have really chosen, based on their own style and budget.

A couple in Texas decided to get married in a week's time. Although they had the means to hold a large reception, they decided because of the time element simply to cater delicatessen food. Friends helped lay out the food, and other friends helped set up a small bar in the groom's home, where both the wedding and reception took place. They had thought of renting a club or restaurant, but decided they would rather celebrate in the home where they would be living. The informality was the deciding factor for them.

Another basic change in the planning of receptions is to divide costs. Traditionally, the bride's parents picked up the entire cost of the reception. But a growing alternative is for both sets of parents to divide the cost (even when it is low), so that no one has to bear the burden of the total expense. When a couple is living away from home, and have no parental support, they most often divide the cost between them. Most people who had managed the cost of their reception on a 50–50 basis said they thought the traditional custom was unfair and outdated. They wanted equality in all things in their marriage right from the start. Certainly not everyone sees the issue this way, but the growing number of couples who are trying to split costs on all wedding expenses indicate that this old custom, too, is changing.

A good example of this change took place at a Kansas wedding recently. The reception was held in the groom's parents' backyard because it was much larger than the bride's parents' yard. Several barbecue ovens were arranged so that guests (about 150) could easily toss a hamburger or small steak on the grill whenever they felt like eating. Salads and other foods were on a large table in the center of the yard. People ate in small groups, then roamed around and socialized. The bride's parents paid for the food, and the groom's parents brought all the liquor and champagne. No one was left with a huge bill, and no one had to stand over a hot fire for hours.

Apart from cost and convenience, receptions have changed because so many people's life-styles have been altered. Values are different. The large sit-down dinner reception that older sister had ten years ago is not as appealing now to many a younger sister or brother. The club or rented hall is less attractive than a private home or outdoor setting. For some, the reality is that marijuana has replaced liquor as the means for relaxation and enjoyment. A group sing may be more popular than a live band. Playing games or sports, for many people, is more fun than standing around drinking champagne or liquor. In many other respects, the change in outlook is reflected in the receptions held by thousands of couples today.

Thus, the underlying spirit of the receptions that

follow personal weddings remains the same as it has been for centuries; what has been altered most is the "sameness" of the affairs. Like the ceremonies that precede them, the personally planned receptions seem to be more original because they have been thought through by the couple. They take place in settings that are more personal. They are less concerned with "perfection" and "impressing the guests" and more interested in celebrating in a way that is comfortable and natural to them. One man summed up the opinions of many people we spoke with: "We put hours of our time into planning our wedding. At first we didn't think much about the reception—we just assumed we'd let someone else take care of it. But after we realized that the wedding would be very special, we decided it would be senseless not to carry that feeling to the reception, too. After all, it was *our* party. We wanted a hand in planning the details. A couple of friends said it would be a hassle to organize it ourselves, and at first it was hard to get everything coordinated. But it really wasn't *that* hard. A lot of friends pitched in and helped us buy food and liquor. A few other friends, and my parents, took care of fixing the food and cleaning up. It wasn't much trouble after all. And it was one hell of a good party, too!"

In addition to the food, the festivities at a reception are also important. In many recent receptions, the ways people have found to entertain themselves and others are, again, more informal than in the past. Whether the party is indoors or outdoors makes a difference. When receptions are held indoors, festivities tend to follow a traditional pattern—dancing, toasting, singing, and socializing. Often, especially when the couple or friends play musical instruments, entertainment is provided by them, either in place of or in addition to professional musicians. We have heard of many games played at wedding parties. One couple showed home movies taken ten years before that included both the bride and groom and several of the guests. We have heard stories of couples involved in sensitivity training and encounter groups bringing some of these elements to the receptions at alternative weddings—nonverbal communication exercises, group activities to bring the two families closer together, group collages to be given as presents to the bride and groom, and so on.

When weddings and receptions are held outdoors, there seems to be more diversity in the activities. In addition to dancing, toasting, and singing, many couples plan other games or sports for everyone to participate in. Group competitive games like softball, volleyball, and football have been played at numerous receptions. Other possibilities are boating, canoeing, swimming, campfires, charades, and drama—all these have been used to allow the guests to celebrate freely, in a relatively unconstrained atmosphere.

Along with food and festivities, two specific and very ancient wedding customs remain in most personal receptions—the bride still throws her bouquet and the guests throw rice at the couple. But even here there have been occasional changes. The old story that the girl who caught the bride's bouquet would be the next to marry has been somewhat deromanticized of late. Many people don't like the presumption that all girls are just dying to "catch a man," as the scramble to catch the bouquet suggests. Thus, at several weddings, brides have been known to toss their flowers, not at a woman, but at a man. It seems like a good way to keep people guessing. Guests, for their part, still throw rice at the couple; but a few alternatives are cropping up even here—like throwing flowers or freeing hundreds of colorful, helium-filled balloons. At one wedding, friends even released a score of doves as the couple left the reception. As the doves disappeared in the distance, the guests also dispersed. It was a memorable and fitting end to a special day.

None of these changes in the alternative wedding reception, neither the surface nor the basic ones, changes the spirit of celebration that has been a part of weddings since time began. Weddings have been, and will continue to be, times of happiness, hope, and rejoicing. Although the range of activities to express this mood seems to be widening, the meaning of this essential part of the wedding remains the same. As one man expressed it to us, "It's the people who make the wedding and reception—not the place, not the food, not the booze. It's being with so many people you love—it's sharing your happiness with them all—that makes weddings and receptions so beautiful." Amen.

SELECTED READINGS

Many volumes and hundreds of articles have appeared in the last decade documenting the changes which were discussed in this chapter. Rather than compiling an exhaustive bibliography, we have selected a few books on each of the themes discussed, as suggested starting points for those who would like to pursue these topics further.

A   On Changing Values and Attitudes

Kenneth Kenniston's *The Young Radicals* (New York: Harcourt, Brace, Jovanovich, 1968) gives an insightful analysis into the backgrounds and motives of many of the young political activists of the 60s. Charles A. Reich's *The Greening of America* (New York: Random House, 1970) and Theodore Roszak's *The Making of a Counter Culture* (New York: Doubleday, 1969) both describe the changing "consciousness" of American society, as viewed from a political, economic, social (and with Roszak a literary) context.

B   On the Changing Church

Martin Marty in *The Fire We Can Light* (New York: Doubleday, 1973) explores the role of religion in a suddenly different world. Fresh insights into the meaning of the Christian Church in the modern world are found in *A New Catechism* (New York: Seabury, 1969, rev. ed.) and Robert F. Hoey's *The Experimental Liturgy Book* (New York: Seabury, 1969) presents more than 100 informal and vital liturgical prayers for today's congregations. In *The New Agenda* (New

York: Doubleday, 1973) Andrew Greeley presents new and controversial proposals for reforming basic religious issues in contemporary and meaningful terms and symbols.

C   On the Women's Movement

In recent years, Betty Friedan's *The Feminine Mystique* (New York: W. W. Norton & Co., 1963) was one of the first and most popular books which described the condition of women in America and gave great impetus to the growing women's movement. Two other books which have done much to awaken the consciousness of American women (and men) are Germaine Greer's *The Female Eunuch* (New York: McGraw-Hill, 1970) and Kate Millet's *Sexual Politics* (New York: Doubleday, 1970).

D   On Changing Styles of Marriage and Relationships

Here are three books that challenge the traditional conception of marriage. They also offer new alternatives for making marriage and other relationships more joyful, equal and growth-facilitating for both parties. George and Nena O'Neill's *Open Marriage* (New York: Evans, 1972) is the most widely known, and the title coined a new term in our culture. Herbert A. Otto compiled an interesting selection of readings in *The Family in Search of a Future: Alternative Models for Moderns* (New York: Appleton-Century-Crofts, 1970). Finally, psychologist-educator Carl R. Rogers' *Becom-*

ing Partners: Marriage and Its Alternatives (New York: Delacorte Press, 1972) offers a fascinating picture of several different styles of marriage and the goals, achievements and conflicts of the persons involved.

4

A Checklist
for Planning
a Personal Wedding

THE CHECKLIST BELOW is provided as an aid
for planning a wedding. It does not look much different from a checklist one might find in any wedding
guide, since most of the *issues* are the same, whether a
wedding is traditional or personal. The real difference
is in how the people make their decisions on each issue.

If you are about to use this list in making your
own wedding plans, we hope you will ask yourselves
one question—and then check the item if your answer
is "yes."

"Have we evaluated the alternatives and made *our
own* choice on this particular issue?"

In formulating the checklist, we tried to cover the
same topics discussed in the text of the handbook.
There are alternatives—dozens of them—for most of
these decisions. You can use the space next to each item
for notes, or to list some of the options you think are
worthy of consideration. We hope you won't feel

bound by the alternatives mentioned in the book, but rather that they will help to generate your own ideas. On some of the issues—attendants or prewedding parties, for example—you may well choose to do nothing. That, too, is a viable alternative. But each issue should at least be considered. After talking over the alternatives available, you will be much more likely to choose options that reflect your own tastes and values and that are truly satisfying to you, both on your wedding day and as you recall the occasion in later years.

Have fun.

1 _____ CHOICE OF DATE

2 _____ LOCATION OF CEREMONY AND RECEPTION

3 _____ TIME OF CEREMONY AND RECEPTION

4 _____ NUMBER AND NAMES OF GUESTS

5 _____ OFFICIANT

6 _____ INVITATIONS

7 _____ DRESS

8   _____ GIFTS

9   _____ ATTENDANTS

10   _____ RINGS

11   _____ PHOTOGRAPHERS, TAPE RECORDING, ETC.

12   _____ FLOWERS

13   _____ DECORATIONS

14   _____ MARRIAGE LICENSE, OTHER LEGAL MATTERS,
NAME CHANGE, ETC.

15   _____ PREWEDDING PARTIES

16   _____ WEDDING PROGRAMS

17   _____ MUSIC AND SINGING FOR CEREMONY

18 _____ PROCESSIONAL AND RECESSIONAL

19 _____ PARTICIPATION OF GUESTS

20 _____ POETRY, PRAYERS, OTHER READINGS

21 _____ VOWS, CONTRACTS, PROMISES

22 _____ FOOD AND DRINK FOR RECEPTION

23 _____ ENTERTAINMENT FOR RECEPTION

24 _____ WEDDING CAKE

25 _____ HONEYMOON

5

The Origins of Marriage

A MAN AND A WOMAN MEET, fall in love, and decide to marry and spend their lives together. We take this story line for granted now, but for our ancestors the institution of marriage was quite different. Two thousand or even two hundred years ago, in most parts of the world, marriages were initiated in ways that are almost completely foreign to us. Today we think in terms of love, respect, compatibility, and need when we think of a marriage partner, but not so in other periods of history. Then the basic ingredients of marriage were strict duty, parental choice, economic necessities, and social approval.

The story of marriage is fascinating because it is central to the history of all human life. In one form or another, marriage has been considered necessary for the survival of any society. The formula is simple: to maintain itself or grow, a group must have children; to have children, men and women must have intercourse; and to have group stability and insure that their children are cared for, a couple must make some bond or com-

Engraving of a Russian Wedding

mitment for the future. This bond of marriage is duplicated on a larger scale. Families join together to form tribes or clans; the latter merge to make villages and towns, then whole nations with a common heritage. The marriage bond contributes to stability and the continuation of the group, and the communal bond is needed for guaranteeing food, shelter, protection from enemies, and commerce. Naturally, each tribe, society, religion, and nation has developed its own customs and laws for marriage. Yet in its most basic form, marriage is the same the world over: it is the approved joining of a man and a woman. They have the right to sexual intercourse and the duty to help and support each other and any offspring they may have. Each society places further demands on the married couple, but essentially their sanctioned right to have sex, plus the obligation to raise children properly, is universal.

Then how has marriage changed? Even though the same duties and rights have been observed since primitive times, the *way* that people have married and how they have led their lives together has altered greatly. Like a child, the institution of marriage has grown and developed through the centuries. It started out as a simple joining of two people, but has become more complex as societies have become more sophisticated and civilized. Many traditions have died away and new ones have replaced them. Important ancient taboos inspired by magical beliefs have given way to strict laws and customs imposed by Church or State. The man at 90 years old is still the same person he was at birth, but changed beyond recognition. So it is with marriage and weddings—the premise is the same today as it was 10,000 years ago, but the social concept of marriage has expanded and altered to remarkable degree since our primitive ancestors were united.

The way people have married through the ages can be divided into three broad categories: marriage by capture, marriage by purchase, and marriage by mutual consent. The first two have almost vanished, at least from our society, but even in marriages based on mutual consent and love, remnants of the traditions of capture and purchase can easily be found.

MARRIAGE BY CAPTURE

Marriage by capture is the oldest form of "marriage." Our idea of the capture is often humorously represented by a picture of a cave man dragging his bride by the hair as she screams in mock protest. The most famous capture marriages in history are probably the carrying away of Helen by Paris of Troy, and the Roman story of the rape of the Sabine women.

Early capture marriages were probably not quite like these myths. Anthropologists generally agree that capturing a mate was never a popular practice, but at certain times, especially during war, men resorted to obtaining women this way. Since from very early times human beings have had strict taboos against incest, a man had to look outside his home or extended family for a mate. In small tribes, he might have to go to other villages to find a marriage partner. If tribes were on good terms, women could be exchanged easily; if not, women were abducted and raped (in Latin, "rape" means "to carry off").

Obviously a culture that condoned the capturing of women could not have held them in very high esteem. Women were basically regarded as slaves whose jobs were to bear children and help with the labor. The more wives a man had, the "wealthier" he was. Before any fixed monetary systems were introduced in the world, a man's wealth was sometimes measured by the number of wives and children he could afford to keep and feed. The majority of societies at any time during history have been patriarchal—men set the rules and laws (in their own favor, of course), and women went along by choice or, more likely, by force. For instance, in many ancient cultures a woman could be traded, captured, divorced with the wave of a hand, killed, lent, or imprisoned for life if she did not satisfy her husband.

Sexual relations were once ruled strictly by magical taboos, and what we call "love" today was very low on the list of priorities. The taboos about women were amazingly strong, for men were really frightened by the "powers" they believed women held. This is one of the major reasons why the laws and customs men invented were weighted so heavily against women: men had to find some way of keeping women in their place. Women were feared because of their power to give birth and because of their menstrual blood. It was widely believed that if a man came in contact with a woman while she was menstruating, he could become ill, die, or lose his "power." So during the menstrual period, women were banished to the outskirts of their villages in order to be far away from men. A woman was also feared during and after pregnancy. In some societies, a man dared not have intercourse with his wife until she had finished nursing the baby—a period lasting anywhere from two to five years. Because of all the taboos, many men kept concubines or other wives for sexual enjoyment as well as procreative purposes.

OTHER PRIMITIVE MARRIAGE STYLES

The most common method of arranging marriages in primitive cultures was the peaceful exchange of wives between tribes. The timing of marriage was usually closely connected to the rites of initiation into the clan. Each boy and girl, at the age of puberty, would become an adult member of the group after certain rites were performed. It was thought that the child literally died and became reincarnated into a new adult through initiation rites, and that this new adult was ready for full membership in the group after he or she showed the ability to conform to the mores and laws of the tribe's elders. Marriage followed shortly after the initiation was completed—although in many societies young people were not totally accepted until they proved they could produce children.

The recent discovery of the Tasaday tribe in the southern Philippines has provided a close look at a society that is comparable to a "stone-age" tribe. These twenty-eight (at last count) people still gather food, use stone tools for labor, and had not planted food or killed wild animals or learned to count until a man from a neighboring tribe taught them. The Tasaday share food communally, but their marriages are strictly monogamous; each man has only one wife, and the couple's children belong to them. In 1972, one Tasaday man, of a marrying age, chose a woman from another tribe to take as his wife. This woman, older and more advanced, accepted, and immediately began living with the Tasaday tribe. Their wedding ceremony was simple. The couple lay on the ground, surrounded by the whole tribe, and gently held and touched each other. A dance was performed, the couple enacted a few other rituals, and the wedding was over.

In primitive cultures, ceremonies such as marriage have always been closely connected with natural rhythms. And nature has been perceived as alive with friendly or malevolent spirits. If the crops failed one year, or if animals were scarce, the tribe believed they had offended the spirits. Nature's cycle of budding, growth, harvest, and dormancy has been seen to be identical to the human life cycle. Marriages, therefore, usually took place in spring or early summer because of the belief that human reproduction was aided by natural cycles. As the crops grew, so would the young bride. Before humans learned that sexual intercourse was the only way to conceive children, they believed that a woman could become pregnant by bathing in a sacred river, walking near a sacred tree, seeing lightning, hearing thunder, or even being exposed to certain winds or rains.

George Thomson describes this connection between nature's cycles and marriage.

Initiations and espousals were accomplished under the control of the whole community. They held their sittings in places set apart from domestic occupation and profane uses. In a wide untrammeled landscape, boys and girls, freed from customary restraints, learnt contact with nature. Waters flowed in the brooks set free by the melting of ice; springs which had been bound by winter burst from the fountains which had once more come to life; the thawed ground opened to let the grass appear; the animals people it, all springing from their retreats. The time of seclusion was over and that of universal interpenetration was come. Earth and sky could commune, and the rainbow was the sign of their union. Closed groups could now enter into alliance, sexual corporations encounter each other. In a landscape which was at once venerable and new, where from time immemorial their ancestors had been at once initiated into social and sexual life, the young people were united.[1]

MARRIAGE BY PURCHASE

Purchase marriage is our most deeply rooted tradition, going back to ancient times and ending—or almost ending—in the West only in the past two hundred years. Even today, our culture retains many effects of this patriarchal custom.

The term "purchase marriage" is sometimes confusing because it is used like an umbrella to cover many different ways of buying a wife or husband. Very

[1] George Thomson, *Aeschylus and Athens*, London: Laurence and Wishart, 1940, p. 123.

simply, it means that some person, service, or commodity was exchanged in gaining a marriage partner. With rare exceptions, it was always the bride who was "sold." She was a valuable piece of property because she was a household worker and childbearer. Purchasing became established as men began to have concern for their own private property. This type of marriage is really not much more than a business contract. Although love probably motivated many marriages, it is fair to say that economics motivated more. A girl's father, knowing the value of a woman, was not content to give her away—he demanded a fair return, most frequently in money, for the loss of his daughter. His daughter, on the other hand, had little to say about the arrangement. She might cry or protest, but unless she was very persuasive, the marriage would go through if her father thought it was a good match. It is not hard to understand, then, why wedding vows, until recently, called for a woman's obedience. The situation also explains why the last name of a woman has been changed, traditionally and legally, from that of her father to that of her husband.

One should not assume that purchase marriages were simple transactions. In most societies they were as complex as a day's proceedings on the New York Stock Exchange. The ritual of marriage followed numerous promises, negotiations, and contracts. The girl's father had to be certain he would be fairly compensated for his daughter, so dealing with a prospective husband or his family was crucial. In most societies, the suitor wanted assurances that the girl was healthy and a virgin. In some cultures the respective families bargained over the price; in others, it was fixed by the elders of the community. In some cases, the most beautiful girls commanded the highest price.

The first type of purchase marriage was probably one of simple exchange—one woman for another. If a man wanted to marry, he would offer his sister or a servant as the "price" for his bride. With this exchange, the father of the bride would not lose a valued worker and the man would gain a wife.

Another type of purchase was the service marriage arrangement. No goods or money changed hands, but a young man would offer himself as a laborer to the woman's father for the promise of eventual marriage. The young man paid for his wife with his sweat. The Old Testament tells of several service marriages, and other literature makes it clear that a man's indenture to his father-in-law could last from one to six or eight years. If, after this time, he had proved himself to be an industrious worker, the father would allow the marriage and the couple could begin to live together.

Child betrothal was another form of purchase marriage. It was a common custom in many countries, particularly in the East. Two families who wished to make a solid bond (usually for economic reasons) would meet when their children were very young. They would decide that one couple's son would marry the other's daughter at the proper time. The children had no voice in the matter, and in many instances did not even meet until shortly before their wedding. This arrangement is still widely practiced in India today, and obviously it is based far more on duty than on love or any other personal feelings.

The most common type of purchase marriage was undoubtedly the "gift" arrangement. Considering how many gifts change hands at a wedding today, it is clear that we have inherited this custom at least in spirit. In its earliest stages, the groom may have simply given his bride's father money or goods on a "cash and carry" basis. The groom might give horses, cows, pelts, or weapons—whatever was valuable in that society. American Indians continued this form of purchase marriage into this century.

Gradually the transaction became more refined. The groom still had to pay, but his expenditure began to be called a "gift" to the father-in-law. The shift in social values did not improve a woman's status, however. Outwardly she was more respected, but she still remained a virtual slave—first to her father, then to her husband.

In many European cultures, a change took place between 500 B.C. and the birth of Christ, a period when the custom grew of supplying the bride with a *dowry*. The practice has lasted into this century. In the dowry marriage, the bride's father supplied her with goods, land, or money so that she could attract a suitable husband. It had, dramatically, become a buyer's market. The groom still gave a gift, but he also received more than just a bride. The dowry was partly a bride's insurance against divorce or her husband's death. But as long as they stayed together, the man controlled the use of the dowry. In essence, it was a gift from father to son-in-law, yet at the same time the dowry made the bride more respected.

Exchange, outright sale, service, child betrothal,

and gift giving were the primary methods for the purchase marriage. With the exception of gift giving, the dowry, and the trousseau, these customs have almost vanished from our culture. But not entirely. Many social assumptions rooted in the concepts of capture and purchase marriage still persist, both in the Western world and elsewhere. In the legal sphere, legislation affecting unwanted pregnancy is an obvious example. From time to time throughout history decisions relating to contraception and abortion, which properly belong in the moral sphere, have been preempted by the State. We forget, too, that women, almost universally, are expected to function as unpaid domestic servants. Although the euphemism "housewife" has gone a long way to obscure the economic contribution made to the gross national product by women working in their own homes, our present economy is dependent on what is, in effect, a vast force of unpaid laborers.

In 1803 the influential British jurist William Blackstone sealed the legal status of married women for decades to come when he set forth in his *Commentaries* the prevailing view that "By marriage the husband and wife are one person in law: that is, the very being and legal existence of the woman is suspended during a marriage." She, her talents, and her assets were legally his. Today several states in the United States still require a married woman to have her husband's permission to enter into certain legal commitments. When a man is being considered for an executive post, especially in government or a large corporation, his wife is frequently scrutinized as carefully as he is. Will she be an asset to him and to his employers?

Will she be able to enhance his prestige by the way she entertains his associates and runs "his" home? In many ways, whether consciously or not, women today are still thought of primarily as childbearers, household workers, and hostesses.

Many of our wedding and marriage standards come to us from Rome, by way of England. In ancient Rome a girl was entitled to her dowry by common law. Her father was compelled to give it in order to help the new couple get started. In the same way today, the bride's family traditionally covers the wedding costs and gives the couple a gift. Even though purchase marriage is no longer an overt part of our culture, many of the customs which had their origins in buying a mate have come down to us in only slightly altered form.

CIVIL AND RELIGIOUS CONTROLS ON MARRIAGE

Marriage and the stability of the family have always been crucial to the growth and strength of a religious group or a nation; both Church and State have attempted to control the laws, mores, and practices of marriage and divorce. Today marriage is governed by civil law and ecclesiastical canon law. Although adherence to canon law depends on one's belief in a particular religion, no one can escape the laws of the State. Most couples celebrate their wedding in the presence of a priest, rabbi, or minister, yet their marriage would be invalid if they did not register it with the State as well.

This was not always so. For centuries the institution of marriage figured in a power struggle between Church and State, and only in the past two hundred years has the civil government of most countries gained the legal authority to license and control marriage.

Historically, the smaller or weaker an organization, the stricter the laws that control the lives of its members. For example, most primitive societies had weak governments but strong magical beliefs. As the mystical "superstitions" began to lose power, they developed into folk customs surrounding the wedding and other ceremonies. These customs were handed down century after century and became the predominant rituals of celebration. The magical meaning was often lost, but the original form of the ritual continued to be used.

Belief in imminent spirits and demons gradually gave way to polytheistic systems where people believed in many gods, each of whom had a specific function and "personality." Greek and Roman gods and goddesses were worshiped as actual beings in the world. One of the most loved and feared was the goddess of marriage; she looked after couples and, of course, was much honored at the wedding ceremony. Ancient Greek weddings were usually celebrated before the altar of the marriage goddess Hera. Since marriage has been seen as a "divine institution" almost from the beginning of time, deities were called upon to bless a union. The idea of the "marriage made in heaven" comes directly from this ancient belief.

As societies became more pluralistic, the State also began to exert control over marriage. Governments of newly formed city-states or nations had to insure stability by codifying laws, and many of the laws concerned the family—the rockbed of the community. So the State began to determine when a couple could marry, who could marry, how the children would be raised, how divorce would be granted, and other legal questions. Since governments and families were run by men, the new State controls over marriage simply perpetuated the age-old belief that women were inferior and dangerous, necessary mainly for bearing children and keeping house.

The Jews were the first people to introduce monotheism. Yahweh, the Hebrew god, was feared and respected above all else; Jewish social and religious codes were inseparable, and marriage laws were strict. Monotheism did not stimulate a revaluation of women, however. In fact, the Old Testament perpetuated for centuries the servile role assigned to women. In Genesis, God fashions man out of the earth and woman is conceived from man's rib. The Adam and Eve story also reinforces the ancient myth that woman is evil, in the control of the devil.

Nor did the birth of Christianity improve woman's position in the home. Despite Jesus' liberal views about women, females were soon relegated to an even lower social and theological level than they were accorded in "pagan" Rome. To a degree extraordinary for his culture, Jesus looked upon women as complete human beings. Man and woman should complement each other perfectly and should always be in harmony, he taught, since marriage is holy. Once married, a couple becomes "one flesh" in the eyes of God; therefore divorce is out of the question. Although Jesus was lofty in his thoughts about marriage, St. Paul and later Church Fathers were less openminded. St. Paul was an advocate of celibacy and had contempt for marriage, calling it a "human frailty." Others viewed marriage as impure and profane because it interfered with the work of devoting one's life to Christ. Women were seen as weak creatures luring men into sin and away from true dedication.

The early Christian attitude was that sex is an evil only to be engaged in for conceiving children. This extreme view resulted in a classic bind: on one hand, exaltation of virginity and chastity; on the other, families with five to fifteen children since methods of birth control were not generally known or allowed. In proclaiming virginity a holy state, the Church Fathers put their theological acceptance on a concept already ages old: since women were regarded as property, men wanted to find them intact. A "used" woman was likened to a broken jar: neither was any good.

The Church had a difficult battle in forcing its conception of "holy matrimony" on Europe because among the ancient European tribes marriage had been governed more by ethnic folk customs than by religious doctrine. Although marriage had its divine aspects, the traditions of the tribe or community counted more—traditions that had been handed down through each generation for many more centuries than the Church had existed. But for hundreds of years the Vatican kept trying. Finally in 1563, at the Council of Trent, the

Church proclaimed that a marriage ceremony not officiated at by a priest who offered the correct ecclesiastical benediction was not valid.

Even after Trent, the question of what made a
marriage official and legal was foggy. Many thousands
of people in Europe over several centuries could not
be certain if their own weddings were valid because of
the continued controversy between Church and State.
Martin Luther made the issue even more complicated
when he declared that marriage should not be in the
domain of the Church, but under civil authority. In
1791 the issue was finally resolved in France in the
constitution that followed the French Revolution. So
that everyone in the country could be treated uni-
formly, the new laws placed marriage under secular
jurisdiction. Canon law was still important, but it no
longer had total control over a couple's decisions about
the age to marry, annulment, or divorce.

The American experience has been different from
the European. Except during the colonial period, the
legal separation of Church and State has been a firm
principle. Although the early settlers imposed strict
religious law on their members, the final authority was
the common law of each colony. Since the adoption of
the federal Constitution in 1787, marriage laws have
been a civil concern, determined by each state legisla-
ture. Although our civil laws on marriage follow English precedent, they have been shaped to a large extent
by the various religious organizations and sects practicing here. It is no wonder, then, that our marriage
and divorce laws vary so much from state to state.

MARRIAGE BY MUTUAL CHOICE

After all the capturing and buying, it has taken society a long time—10,000 years at the very least—to embrace marriage based on mutual consent and love as a mass practice. Instead of having one's husband or wife chosen, a person is freer today than at any time in history to marry because of feelings of love and personal need.

With the rise of capitalism and the birth of the Industrial Revolution in Europe and America in the nineteenth century, new industries began taking over work traditionally done by women: weaving, candle-making, bread making, sewing, soap making, and many other tasks. Instead of each family being responsible for its own goods, the larger society took over. Furthermore, with the growing need for cheap labor, women gradually took jobs in the new industries. For the first time in history on any large scale, women began to achieve economic independence. With this independence, small as it was at first, also came the beginning of the freedom of choice.

The changes didn't occur overnight. But capitalism brought about broad social and moral alterations that are now clearly evident, including the decline of the traditional male-dominated household. Women left many of their domestic duties and went off to work in factories and offices. The State affected the home even more by taking over children's education, giving women still greater mobility. As the State's authority rose, religious organizations began to lose their power over much of the population; divorce became possible, and for the first time since antiquity women were able to terminate their marriages.

Capitalism has brought about a general decline in male dominance within the home. When women did not *have* to be household servants, they began, finally, to be seen as individuals. They, like men, had choices to make—about where to live, how to live, when and whom to marry. Women were able to begin to feel that love, sexual activity, and personal happiness were more important in marriage than the dependence their foremothers had known. Though men have always assumed the right for themselves, women were now in a position to find and have a "self." Marriage by mutual choice, with both partners having distinct identities, became a reality.

And so the rituals and traditions of marriage are slowly changing. During most of this century, couples have taken wedding vows hundreds of years old, using words that reflect a world long past. Now many of the old customs are being replaced by practices that have more immediate meaning for those getting married.

Weddings are only part of the changing picture. With women achieving greater equality in all areas of life, alternative forms of living patterns are becoming widespread. Today we see the "American Dream" being sought in many ways. Experiments in communal living, intentional communities, the extended family, living together without formal marriage, "contract marriage" and "open marriage" are becoming increasingly frequent. Just as the "old" wedding is not sufficient for many, the "old" life styles are not the only answer for people looking forward to the twenty-first century.

Capture, purchase, choice. The evolution has been long and slow. And as long as people seek alternatives that fit their own needs, reflect their desires, and help them lead happier lives, many more changes will come in the future.

SELECTED READINGS

For those who want a more complete study of the history of marriage, dozens of books are available, though they are mainly housed in large libraries. We have selected several of the most interesting ones here. In many cases, the authors disagree bitterly about the origins of marriage, and the reader recognizes quite clearly that there are few solid facts, but many interpretations, concerning the "art of marriage."

If you are very interested, and have a lot of time, the two most complete studies are George Elliott Howard's *A History of Matrimonial Institutions* (Chicago: University of Chicago Press, Callegan and Company, 1904. 3 volumes), and the classic by Edward Westermarck, *A History of Human Marriage* (London: Macmillan and Company, 1891. 3 volumes, 5th ed., 1921).

There are also numerous shorter works on the subject. The anthropologists Robert Briffault and Bronislaw Malinowski debate the origins of marriage in *Marriage Past and Present* (ed. by M. F. Ashley Montagu, Boston: P. Sargent, 1956). Briffault offers his ideas about the importance of women in society in *The*

Mothers: The Matriarchal Theory of Social Origins (Abridged. New York: Universal Library, 1963). Margaret Cole's *Marriage Past and Present* (New York: J. M. Dent and Sons Ltd., 1938), and Ernest Crawley's *The Mystic Rose* (London: Macmillan and Company Ltd., 1902), are enjoyable and often humorous accounts of how marriage may have developed on this planet. Other excellent shorter studies include Franz Muller-Lyre's *The Evolution of Modern Marriage* (New York: Alfred A. Knopf, 1930), Ralph de Pomerei's *Marriage Past Present and Future* (New York: Richard R. Smith, 1930), and Westermarck's *A Short History of Marriage* (New York: Macmillan Company, 1926).

The pioneering work in the anthropological study of human relationships and their world of mystic belief is Sir James Frazer's *The Golden Bough*. Although the original work is dense and very long, there is an excellent abridgment of his work called *The New Golden Bough,* edited by Theodore H. Gaster (Garden City, New York: Doubleday Anchor Books, 1959). Havelock Ellis is another early explorer in the field of marriage and the evolution of society. His *Marriage Today and Tomorrow* (San Francisco: Westgate Press, 1929) is the best of his works. Finally, Robin Fox's *Kinship and Marriage: An Anthropological Perspective* (Harmondsworth, England: Penguin, 1967), and Claude Levi-Strauss's *The Elementary Structures of Kinship* (Boston: Beacon Press, 1969), offer highly detailed and fascinating reading about the origins of the family and the institution of marriage.

6

The Roots
of Wedding Ritual

TOM AND ALICE fell in love and decided to get married. After Tom asked Alice's father permission for her hand, the couple went to their minister to tell him the good news. The couple and their parents made up a guest list. Tom asked his best friend, George, to be his best man. Alice asked Janet to be her maid of honor. On the wedding day, Alice and her father walked down the church aisle and the minister asked, "Who gives this woman to be married to this man?" Alice's father nodded and gave his daughter's hand to Tom. The couple repeated their vows, exchanged rings, and waited for the minister's words, "I pronounce you man and wife." As Tom lifted the veil to kiss Alice, the guests gave a sigh of happiness and relief. It was over. They were married! Then the couple left the church in a sprinkle of rice and were driven off to a reception. They ate and danced, cut the wedding cake, and Alice threw her bouquet to one of the young women in the crowd. After the festivities, Tom and Alice left on their honeymoon.

A very familiar story, isn't it? But what will surprise most people is that *all* the rituals in Tom's and
Alice's wedding are thousands of years old—rituals that
were devised in times when belief in magical or mystical powers was extraordinarily strong. All of these
customs—rings, vows, rice, etc.—have been passed
from generation to generation for centuries; and even
though some of them have lost their original intent,
the form has survived.

Before human beings had rational or scientific
answers to the questions that were most important to
them—Why does it rain? What is the sun? Why do
women have babies? Where do we go when we die?—
they made up answers that made sense to them. The
reliance on magic can be seen in the myths of all cultures. Yet to those who were ruled by these ideas,
what we call "myths" today were very serious lessons.
Stated simply, early people believed that they were the
recipients of good or evil from the powers in the universe; they could not control these powers, but they
could help or defend themselves by adhering to prescribed rituals. If they made the "right" gesture or followed the "right" course of action at a given time, then
things would turn out in their favor; if not, big trouble
was ahead.

People of all ages and cultures are superstitious.
Even in our highly rational times (from a historical
viewpoint at least), superstitions abound. Try to find
the thirteenth floor of a New York office or apartment
building—it usually isn't there because it has been
numbered fourteen instead. Or make a date with
someone for Friday the thirteenth; or walk under a

ladder, break a mirror, or say the wrong thing and watch for people's responses. Superstitions may seem foolish and out-dated, but there are millions in the world who still live their lives ruled by them. Imagine what it was like before rational answers could be worked out for many of the questions we still ask today.

For our ancestors, the three major events in life (and therefore the events that had the most rituals attached to them), were birth, marriage, and death. And all three were intimately related. Childbirth was surrounded by the omnipresent danger of death for mother or child, so it was an occasion for rejoicing when it was successful. Marriage also had aspects of joy and sorrow, an awesome occasion, suggesting all the fearful mysteries of life and death that preceded and followed it. So it is not difficult to understand why so many rituals and customs concerned with weddings were cloaked in magical vestments.

But why have these rituals lingered on for so long? The rituals described in this chapter were devised thousands of years ago. What do we have in common with people of those ages? What is so mystical today? On the surface, the whole world has changed; yet some mysteries remain constant for all humans. The mystery of love, of deep feelings for another person; the fear of the unknown in the future, the unknown in another person; the hope for a good life, the promise of commitment—these emotions are the same in us as they undoubtedly were for the people who invented the rituals in the past. We all have different ways of expressing love, hope, or fear, but the rituals on the following pages, and the new ones being performed today, all give form to emotions in a way that everyone can understand. After many performances, they become part of a culture, handed down from one generation to the next, unquestioned.

According to the best information we could gather, these are how many of our wedding customs originated.

THE BEST MAN: The fellow we now call the best man probably began his duties by acting as a guard or decoy for a friend who intended to capture a wife. The groom brought along one or more friends to protect him from the girl's angry tribesmen. In those days marriage was a simple ceremony: once the groom had snatched his bride out of her village, they were considered "married." The wedding was the abduction itself, with the best man serving as witness, thereby making it "legal." The best man's functions didn't stop there. Usually the new husband had to appease his bride's family, so the best man was sent as an envoy for the groom, carrying gifts to soothe them.

During the long period of purchase marriage, the best man and the groomsmen often served as intermediaries between the prospective groom and his future bride's family. The best man could carry messages, deliver the purchase booty, arrange the ceremony, and even escort the young woman to the ceremony to insure her safety. He served both as good friend and lawyer for the groom. If a wedding was unpopular with some people in a community, the best man's role was more dangerous. He had to carry a weapon to protect the new couple from harm. During the Italian Renaissance, several marriages between families of nobility upset the townsfolk. In Florence, for example, one couple had to be surrounded by friends who fought off the angry crowds as the couple left the church after the ceremony.

The best man is still a helper for the groom, but his functions are now more social than military. He's needed as a legal witness for the wedding and usually signs the marriage certificate. At a traditional wedding he usually makes arrangements for the groom and carries the wedding ring at the ceremony. But probably the most enduring reason for retaining the best man tradition is friendship. A groom usually chooses a close friend or relative to stand by his side at the wedding —to bolster his courage or calm his nerves. Since a wedding is such an important event, sharing it with a long-time friend creates a further bond between the two. Choosing a best man is a symbolic way of saying, "You are a true friend. Stand with me and help me, and share the joy of my wedding."

THE MAID OF HONOR: In very early societies, many fears and taboos surrounded a young woman about to be married. Because she was considered highly vulnerable to evil spirits, she had to be closely watched by other women of the tribe and actively avoided by all the men. Many tribes isolated a bride-to-be in a hut some distance from the village, where she might be interned for as long as a month. This served as a purification rite and kept the male members of the tribe from supposed danger.

The banished woman's best friend or closest relative looked after her, supplying food and attending to her other needs. It was believed that if demons were in the air, the bride's friend would be able to scare them away, for although the bride was vulnerable, the friend was not.

As in the case of the best man, some vestiges of these important duties may have clung to the bride's chief attendant down through the ages. Essentially, however, the bride, like the groom, turns for support to a close friend or relative saying, in effect, "I want you to be with me on this important day."

BRIDESMAIDS AND GROOMSMEN: The bridesmaids and groomsmen, or ushers, are simply extensions of the basic roles of the maid of honor and best man. Their function in weddings today is mainly symbolic, a holdover from ancient times when more than one friend was needed to capture or protect.

Ushers help in large weddings by seating guests and keeping order, and this role, too, has roots far back in time. In most primitive societies the fear of evil spirits of all shapes and forms was so pervasive that many wedding rituals were invented as appeasement of these spirits on such an important day. One way to protect the couple was to have a select group of people surround them at the ceremony. This is probably the reason for the formation of the "wedding party" as we know it today. But some cultures went even farther in their attempt to shield the couple from evil. If the groom wore black clothing, then all the groomsmen wore black, too. If the bride wore white, her brides-

maids dressed the same way. Why? Because if everyone looked alike, then the evil spirits would not be
able to tell anyone apart, and therefore would not
know who the *real* bride and groom were! Thus, the
tradition today of having all the bridesmaids in the
same dress and all the groomsmen in tuxedos or dark
suits is not just for aesthetic reasons, but probably is
a direct holdover from the days of magic when this
trick was used to thwart the evil eye. If you've ever sat
through a formal wedding at which you did not know
the groom well, you'll agree that it is difficult to tell
him apart from four or five groomsmen all dressed in
the same attire.

Groomsmen have been asked to perform some
other strange services in the past. In some ancient cultures where sexual intercourse was considered very
dangerous and mysterious, the new husband would not
be the first to sleep with his bride because of the risk
involved in breaking the hymen and causing her to
bleed. So the best man or one of the groomsmen would
have intercourse with her first, causing any evil spirits
to descend upon the less vulnerable friend. Or the
groomsmen would stay in the room with the couple as
they had intercourse, just to make sure nothing bad happened. (These seem to be two customs that have *not*
endured through the ages.) In other societies, groomsmen were selected to enter the couple's home immediately after the ceremony to frighten away any spirits
that might be lying in wait. One method was to build
a fire and smoke them out; or the groomsmen would
go to the couple's bed and carefully search underneath
it.

Our present tradition of having a wedding party is inherited directly from early Roman times. Then the party protected the couple's money and belongings as well as playing an active part in the ceremony. This custom has been retained through the centuries as a practical act of keeping the couple secure from danger.

Many couples who plan personal weddings question the need for a wedding party of any kind. Instead of selecting a few friends to stand symbolically apart from all the other guests, some couples simply consider all guests as participants in the ceremony. The need for a best man, maid of honor, or a formal wedding party is based solely on tradition, and as couples set out to make their weddings more to their own style or taste, many find this is one custom that can be left in the past.

RINGS: When a man and woman exchange rings at their wedding, they are symbolically sealing a bond of unity. It's a very personal, private moment for the couple; the rings represent the promises they have made in their wedding. But the ring is also a public symbol. A wedding ring on a man or woman's fingers tells the world that a person is spoken for, unavailable. It is a universal symbol, understood by all. The dual role of wedding symbols—rings, tattoos, jewelry, skin cuttings, or certain clothing—is as old as marriage. Each society devises some way of showing unity between two people, and whether it is the ring given today or the weeds that primitive couples tied around their wrists thousands of years ago, the meaning is identical.

The most ancient and universal symbol of the marriage union was holding hands. In many cultures a couple could not hold hands until they were officially wed. Even if a wedding contained no verbal vows, the simple act of hand holding was often enough to make the marriage valid. And since antiquity, holding hands, if only to exchange rings, has been part of almost every marriage service on earth. Today we have rings, legal certificates, and vows to show the world a couple is married, but the natural, affectionate hand holding by a couple in love still says much more.

The tradition of giving an engagement ring to the future bride dates back to ancient times when purchase marriage was the norm. When a young man went looking for a wife, he had to deal with her father. Generally the two men would discuss the terms, and the suitor was then responsible for conveying part of the price before the wedding. In early cultures, a young woman might have been valued at the worth of ten cows and a certain portion of the yearly crop. The young man might have given the woman's father five cows with the promise of full payment on the day of the wedding. This down payment later became known as "earnest money." It was a respected and necessary part of any wedding negotiation.

Before paper and coin currency were invented, money was reckoned in precious metals as well as livestock or land. Most people kept their liquid assets in the form of ornaments to be worn, often in the shape of a ring so the money could be kept on a person's body. A young suitor's "earnest money" was then delivered in the form of one or more finger rings. The young woman's father got the rings at first, but slowly the tradition developed that money was given to the father, and the symbolic ring to the bride-to-be.

It's easy to see how these traditions have come down to us today. In early Anglo-Saxon times a marriage contract had two distinct parts. First was the "beweddung" or betrothal, which was really the sale of the bride. "Beweddung" means "buying a maid." In this part, the suitor paid his earnest money to the woman's father and set the date for the wedding itself. The second part, "gifta," was the actual marriage ceremony—which, of course, took place only after the full price had been paid. In most of Europe, silver coins were the most common payment. After the blatant purchase marriage fell out of favor, the custom of giving something of value to the woman's father still persisted. In fact, up until this century it was proper for a young man to offer a symbolic silver coin to his future father-in-law. And although we don't think of purchase when a man gives his fiancée an engagement ring today, the original intent of "sealing the bargain" still lingers.

The wedding ring symbolizes a "binding union" in marriage—but in earlier centuries, the binding was literal. In many cultures, a central part of the wedding ceremony consisted of tying some object on the bride and groom. Some tribes used grass, weeds, animal skins, hair, or other natural materials. In one tribe, rings of grass were tied on each partner, and later in the ceremony the rings were joined, binding the two together until the wedding was over. Along with hand holding, tying some object to both bride and groom appears to have been a universal practice. Even into the nineteenth century in several European countries a couple's hands were bound together all through their wedding. What better way can one think of for advertising a marriage than having two people roped together?

But the ring offered at the wedding has other meanings as well. It has symbolized union and love, but also enslavement and inferiority. Throughout most of early Western history, the wedding ring represented a man's control over his wife. As often as we hear fabulous love stories of ancient times, we now know they are more myth than reality, especially for common folk of any land. It would be romanticizing history too much to think that the wedding ring has always been the symbol of divine unity or equal comradeship.

Thousands of different rings have been used as wedding rings. Silver and gold bands have been in existence since ancient Egyptian and Greek times. They were the most precious metals available, and so the best suited for symbolizing the worth of marriage. Diamonds and other stones have also been set in rings for thousands of years. Each stone represents a quality or emotion, and many early wedding rings were covered with gems. During Medieval and Renaissance times, the signet ring replaced gold bands as wedding rings. The signet ring was a man's seal of ownership or authority, so passing his ring to his bride at the wedding also had the same meaning: he controlled her. To make matters worse, the man also gave her the household keys at the ceremony, thus reminding her she had many duties ahead. It was a not very subtle way of saying that the woman's place was in the home.

The custom of exchanging rings at the wedding

has a long history, too. In most Northern European countries, the original tradition of tying a knot of rope between the bride and groom at the ceremony was replaced by the breaking of a gold coin, one half going to the husband, the other half to the wife. The custom clearly represents purchase, but it also was a way of showing that the two people must stay together to increase their "value." Centuries later the coin breaking was dropped in favor of the custom we have inherited —each partner giving a ring to the other so that both can wear the gift of their wedding day.

The belief that a ring is a symbol of unending love dates back to the days of Egyptian Pharaohs. They thought the ring signified an "endless indissoluble union," an endless circle that forever feeds into and nourishes itself. Christians also see the ring as the representation of the perfect union—man and woman united as one in matrimony. The ring symbolizes fidelity, perfection, a sacred bond, trust, and, of course, love. With all these associations, it's no wonder the tradition has lasted so long.

Why does almost everyone choose the third finger, left hand for the wedding ring? An interesting myth is responsible for the choice of this finger. Ages ago it was believed that a certain vein ran directly from this finger to the heart, thus the third finger was closest to the seat of love. Apparently this was an accepted truth for many centuries, and the custom was never questioned. Medical science has proved that no such vein exists; but the tradition is so ingrained that changing it now would be almost impossible. During the Elizabethan period, English women favored their thumbs for wedding rings, but the custom was short lived.

And why the left hand? That's basically a matter of convenience, too. Most people are right-handed, and when wedding rings were very large, as in ancient times, they could prove to be a nuisance. So the third finger of the left hand was the most practical place to wear the ring to keep it out of the way.

WEDDING DISGUISES: Marriage has always been regarded as a risky enterprise, and it still is today. In periods when belief in magical systems was strong, people thought that whatever took place on the wedding day, good or bad, could color the whole future of the marriage. If a bad omen or an evil spirit was seen, the couple's happiness or number of children was thought to be doomed or in jeopardy. Because of these beliefs, couples had to take numerous precautions to minimize the danger. But the real differences between our ancient ancestors and ourselves is that they firmly believed they had *no control* over what happened to them—they were totally at the mercy of impersonal forces. Today we know we have more control over our own lives, so many of the rituals designed to thwart evil seem absurd to us. Yet we are still plagued with many of the same uncertainties and fears that early people suffered; we simply handle them in a different way.

Marriage today is as mysterious and precarious as it was 3,000 years ago. Many couples planning personal weddings try consciously to cleanse their ceremonies of the old ways of dealing with doubt and unknowns. By confronting the uncertainties directly in the ceremony, with vows, contracts, or promises, couples today are trying to achieve more control over their married lives, leaving less to fate or the whims of the gods.

The following rituals are all of ancient origin, yet they have survived in many varieties because of superstition and tradition. Some of them are now almost obsolete, and with the rising consciousness about weddings and marriage, the bridal veil has already lost its appeal for most women. Hiding or disguising the bride and groom to keep them from danger does not appear to be the wave of the future.

In parts of India, an old custom had the bride dress up as a boy while another girl took her place as the "bride" for the ceremony. The groom stood nearby, protected by his entourage. In this case the spirits were supposed to descend on the substitute girl so the real couple could escape harm. In ancient Greece the opposite ritual was often used. The groom dressed as a girl and he and his bride went through the ceremony looking—they hoped—identical. Probably the best disguise recorded is the one where both bride and groom were covered from head to toe in ceremonial carpets. If that didn't protect them, nothing would—but this practice made it difficult for guests to comment on "what a lovely couple" they made.

Dressing in the opposite sex's clothing was a frequent custom in primitive societies. The deep-seated fears and taboos about the other sex can be clearly seen in these rituals; disguise was used not only to prevent outside harm, but also to lessen the dangers and mystery of sex itself. By exchanging clothing, the bride and groom would symbolically be in the other's "place" for a while, thus gaining some magical familiarity with his or her powers. Edward Westermarck, author of the authoritative *History of Human Marriage,* compares this custom to an inoculation shot. People who observed the custom were really trying to achieve a mystical knowledge of the persons they were marrying. Sex was frightening, and these early ancestors of ours were playing out a ritual that has since been described and explained by Freud and others—the "loved one" was also the "dreaded one." Attraction and repulsion were mixed together in the disguise custom more intricately than in almost any other wedding tradition. The partner is trusted and loved, but also hated and feared because each sex possesses traits mysterious to the other. Men feared women's powers to conceive and bear children. Women feared men's physical strength and authority in the society. By changing places with each other at the wedding it was hoped that some of these troubling differences might be neutralized.

During the Middle Ages, Eastern Jews switched clothing, but they also went a bit further to protect themselves. The bride, dressed as a man, donned helmet and sword just in case spirits might be lurking around. The safest ploy of all was used in several parts of Asia and the Near East. A married couple would literally serve as decoys at the altar for the bride and groom; they would go through all the rituals and motions of being married in order to attract demons to themselves. The real bride and groom would hide. This last custom points out that disguising was serious business, and not the slightest chance could be taken on one's wedding day. The spirits of danger (and, of course, the psychological unknown) were respected with the utmost attention and deference.

VEILS: Bridal veils have a long and complicated history. The custom of covering the bride's face on her wedding day is widespread, recorded in numerous societies around the world. The first instances of veiling were undoubtedly to protect the vulnerable new bride from the evil eye. Because the woman was regarded as weaker and more prone to danger, she was usually the one to be veiled. The tradition lingered on for centuries until it became an expected practice. Christians changed the custom to a representation of a woman's innocence and purity, and it is in this form that we have inherited the custom.

In Moslem countries, women have always been regarded as servants. Until recently, women kept their faces veiled at most times throughout their whole lives (some still do), since only her husband is supposed to see a woman's face uncovered. In this case the veil is a symbol of submission and servitude, and many anthropologists believe that the wedding veil also had its origins in the same attitude of male domination.

Veils have also been used to protect another kind of secret. When weddings had been arranged by the couple's parents, and the bride and groom had never seen each other, the girl wore a veil throughout the ceremony. These marriages were negotiated in childhood, and when the right time came the couple had no choice but to fulfill their parents' wishes. After the ceremony was completed the husband would lift his new bride's veil and see her face for the first time.

Still other variations on the theme of hiding the

bride have been observed. In some Near East lands, a curtain was placed between the couple all through the ceremony so they could not see or touch each other until officially united. This practice is really a more elaborate form of veiling in which the whole body of both bride and groom is hidden from the other. These customs, which were originally intended to save the couple from bad luck or the evil eye, later led to the superstition that bad things would happen to the bride and groom who saw each other on their wedding day before the ceremony. In many countries, the couple was kept from seeing one another for as much as two or three days before the ceremony. Elaborate precautions were carried out to prevent them from laying eyes—or hands—on each other.

Certainly magic isn't the only issue here. Bad luck is one thing, but what all these customs may also indicate is that the bride and groom had to be restrained from seeing each other because their sexual passion was so high. Taboos against seeing or touching a loved one are based on conflicting feelings—desire for and fear of someone close. Thus separating the couple before the wedding, and veiling the bride during it, lessened the possibility that a couple might break a rule or taboo of the society.

CUTTING HAIR: Cutting the bride's hair was once a common practice from Europe to China, and it had two distinct meanings attached to it. The primary reason for shearing the bride's hair was undoubtedly to disguise her. But the other motive was to show that the woman had a new position in life—that of a wife.

In most societies it was, and is still, acceptable for

a single girl to wear long flowing hair. But when she gets married, something else is expected. This transition points clearly to the sexual implications of hair and how it is worn. Long, unbound hair is associated with youth and freedom. But the minute a young woman married—off came the hair. Early church fathers decreed that women must always cover their heads while inside a church since hair was considered a provocative adornment, bringing out lust in men and therefore unseemly in a place of worship.

Cutting hair is also connected with the idea of loss of power, so it is not strange that the woman was the one to be clipped. She was the "feared one" in primitive societies, the one whose powers had to be neutralized and kept in check. Add to this belief the need for disguise, and you have a full-blown tradition that still exists in many countries. In Sparta, in the fifth century B.C., a girl's hair was cut to resemble her husband's before the wedding. Then she dressed like a boy for the ceremony so that both of them looked alike. In the Orient the custom was to shave the bride's eyebrows to tell the community of her new position— but also to make her unattractive to other men who might desire her.

MOCK WEDDINGS: In most families, the older children marry first. Women are very often younger than the men they marry, so if a girl weds while her older brother is single, no one thinks much of it. But if a girl marries at nineteen and her older sister is still unattached, the older sister is apt to take a good deal of kidding from friends. Some cultures didn't look on this as a laughing matter. For millions of people in India and throughout the Far East, marriage of children has to be in order of birth. It was a custom sanctioned by religious codes.

What happened when a boy wanted to marry before his older brother was engaged? South Indians came up with the perfect solution; marry the elder to a tree, a rock, or some other inanimate object. It seems a bit far-fetched to modern Westerners, but this type of mock marriage was performed with great seriousness. Trees were believed to be inhabited by real spirits, so the bond between a human being and a tree was actually a union with a live, benevolent god. It is a belief common to all early societies and is generally called animism or totemism. One particular object, a tree or animal, would become the totem, or sacred object, for a tribe. A "marriage" to this respected totem would clear the path for a younger sibling to marry a human, thereby side-stepping the obligation to wed in chronological order. The elder brother could later marry a human, but in India, even up to this century, the person married to the totem often became a priest for the object and never married.

Mock marriages had another function, too. Totem marriages were often performed in the hope that evil could be diverted into the tree or animal. A man would wed a tree first, making the spirits attack the safe object; then he could marry his human partner. Westermarck cites a marvelous example of the mock wedding. In one mid-Eastern country, a sheep was dressed up like the bride and led around a sacrificial fire in order to fool the evil eye. The real bride hid in the distance to make certain all was safe. Then the groom was actually married to the sheep while the woman looked on from the bushes. If demons struck, only the sheep was doomed.

Luckily for us, times and values change. So if you have an older brother, yet unmarried, you can assure him he won't have to be married to the family Ford before you go ahead with your plans.

DANGERS BENEATH THE GROUND AND IN THE AIR: Our early ancestors seem to have come up with rituals for almost every possible danger a couple might encounter on their wedding day. Bad tidings could come from anywhere—the sky or the earth. To protect the couple from demons in the ground, many primitive societies came up with the logical solution: carry the bride and groom around all day until the ceremony was over. If the bride and groom never touched the bare earth they were thought to be relatively safe.

Some tribes believed that women were more endangered than men, and only women were carried. A common ritual still in use in many parts of the world today consists in transporting the bride to and from the ceremony in a painted wagon or litter. In most places animals were used, but sometimes the husband carried his bride on his back. This custom shows a measure of respect, but it was devised primarily to protect the couple's future happiness.

Nor has comparable ritual completely disappeared. In formal weddings today, a red or white carpet is sometimes rolled out just before the ceremony for the bride to walk on as she makes her way to the altar. In other countries, flowers are thrown, or leaves or animal skins are used to honor the path of the bride. We know it as the "red carpet treatment," an obvious way of showing respect for someone special, as the bride certainly is on her wedding day. But, as usual, most people who carry out this ritual have no idea of its original purpose.

Another familiar gesture that stems directly from the ancient fear of demons in the ground is the custom of carrying the bride over the threshold of the couple's new apartment or home. It's usually done in mock fashion today because this ritual has been used so often by Hollywood movie directors that it has, like so many others, become a cliché.

The custom arose out of the universal superstition about entering new places. The new, the unknown, the future, have always been mysterious. People in all times have believed in prophets and seers, those blessed souls who could (perhaps) see into the future and report on it to relieve some of the fear in common folk. The popularity of astrology, the I Ching book, Jeane Dixon, and Edgar Cayce depend on our fascination with the future. No matter how technologically and scientifically sophisticated a society may become, these fears, and their antidotes, will continue.

For a newly married couple, the threshold of a house or room was a particularly dangerous place. The threshold was the "future," and it might harbor evil spirits. It's an easy belief to understand. Think of walking into a dark house or room—most of us *do* hesitate at the door, a little afraid of what might be inside. So the vulnerable bride would be carried across the threshold to keep her from harm on her wedding day.

Another interpretation to this ritual is equally sound: Like so many other marriage customs, it can be seen as just another instance of the "dominant male–passive female" stereotype that keeps men and women from truly being partners. Throughout most of Western history, women have been seen as second-class citizens, so the gesture of carrying a woman into a new house certainly does call up images of a master-servant relationship. The custom also harks back to the practice of capturing and carrying away a bride.

The magical and authoritarian aspects of carrying a bride over the threshold have been almost forgotten by our time. It's thought of now as a rather romantic ritual, one that causes stammering, foot shuffling, and many protests—yet one that is often seen because so many people think it's "part of the pageant."

Everybody loves a parade, and the small parade of a newly married couple usually attracts attention. Their vehicle is often painted "Just Married!" or is decorated with ribbons and streamers (another custom thousands of years old). Or, more noticeably, the car is trailing a string of empty cans. It's a merry sight, and a noisy one, too.

All the honk and clatter are certainly part of the celebration, another way a couple can publicize their marriage and draw less involved bystanders into their joy for a moment or two. But noisemaking once served a very different purpose. Along with other preventive rituals, making loud noises throughout a wedding ceremony was simply another method of keeping evil spirits at bay.

The people who initiated the noise-making practices obviously believed that their frightening sounds would help drive demons away. From early primitive times, drums, horns, bells, sticks—anything to produce noise—would be rounded up for a wedding. When we see films of tribal cultures in different parts of the world today, all this noise seems merely festive. That's certainly part of the ritual, but even in this century the primary function is intended to be protection. We have inherited the ritual, but not the original intent. Somehow playing Wagner's 'Wedding March' or a song by the Beatles doesn't conjure up images of warding off the evil spirits.

The most popular deterrent among the people of Europe and the Near East was firing guns and rifles. As the bride and groom were being married, their attendants—and usually anyone else in the crowd—stood around them firing rounds of ammunition into the air. This sounds rather disconcerting to us today, especially because it would be hard to hear the ceremony; but the practice lasted for centuries. The presence of weapons like daggers, rifles, swords, and whips was taken for granted at wedding ceremonies; they were intended to safeguard the couple from the supernatural and to discourage worldly outlaws from coming too close to the wedding gifts.

FIRE AND WATER: In very early ages, when little scientific knowledge had been acquired, fire and water were regarded with great respect and deference. Most primitive societies had gods or goddesses of fire and water. Today, fire and water are still basic to many rituals. Babies are baptized in water; candles usually burn in temples, churches, and mosques; cremation of the dead is a custom thousands of years old.

Fire and water have also been used in wedding ceremonies in numerous ways through the centuries. Together or separately, they were tools to keep away demons and to cleanse the participants of any evil that might be in or on their bodies. Women of the Moslem faith must ritually bathe before their weddings; so must orthodox Jewish women. In ancient Greece, women purified themselves before a wedding by bathing in a river or fountain holy to the goddess of wedlock. Even in modern Greece, water is part of the ceremony: hands and feet are washed to insure purity. It is easy to see how the ancient custom of washing off evil spirits evolved and was adopted by major religions and changed in emphasis to symbolize "washing away evil."

Fire has been used even more elaborately in wedding ceremonies. Its original function was to "light the darkness" and dispel evil. Huge torches used in the past have their modern equivalents in the custom of burning candles. In ancient Greece and Rome, the bride was usually escorted to and from the wedding in a procession of torches. In fact, fire was even regarded as a legitimate "witness" to a marriage in Greece. A wedding without the presence of a torch fire was not considered fully sanctified. Fire was not a simple ornament or light-giving element—it bordered on the supernatural. The powers of darkness were believed to harbor evil spirits, so the function of the torches was both elemental and spiritual. Torches split the darkness and made demons recede, thereby purifying the air and surrounding space. Even in the daytime torches were used in wedding processionals.

In Russia, centuries ago, one custom was to form a large pile of straw inside the house where the wedding would take place. The straw was then burned so that all the demons would be scared away before the ceremony. It must have been rather hard on the floors, but apparently the trick was successful. Candles or small torches will probably always be a part of weddings because of their romantic qualities. Nevertheless, all of us who marry surrounded by candles or gas torches are also playing out another universal and ancient ritual.

CANOPIES: Noises, torches, and ritual baths were not always considered enough protection from the air. In several countries around the world one also finds the custom of covering the heads of the bride and groom. Umbrellas, scarves, hats, and canopies have been the most widely used protectors. In Jewish weddings, the couple stands under a canopy, or *chuppah,* during the ceremony. This is an ancient ritual, to honor and protect the bride and groom. It also symbolically establishes a house in public to represent that their lives will be spent together. In older times, four men would generally hold up the *chuppah* on sticks, thus surrounding the pair to insure greater safety. The Chinese used an umbrella in much the same way. Other cultures relied on wearing hats all through the day of the wedding.

Covering the head was originally a magical practice which our ancient ancestors thought would protect them from irrational happenings caused by supernatural forces; our later ancestors, when forming institutional religions, copied the practice but changed the meaning. Thus, the Christian woman and Jewish man who cover their heads while in church or synagogue are not "protecting" themselves, but showing respect for God. The magical element of the custom has been changed to a ritual of respect for the divine. When all the early religious communities formed, they borrowed the rites and customs of their predecessors, then enlarged on them, formed their own more logical systems, and gave their own meanings to the older customs. The world's major religions have a great deal in common, even though on the surface each seems very different. The most striking area of commonality is how each religion drew heavily upon the rituals and physical symbolism of mystical societies before them.

RITUALS OF LUCK: Most of the rituals we've seen so far have had their origins in preventing something disastrous from happening to the bride and groom. But there are just as many customs that promote festivity and rejoicing. A wedding is a happy time, and it always has been. No social function generates as much general joy in a community as the marriage of two of its members.

Until this century, life revolved primarily around the extended family or small community, and a marriage was an event that usually involved many members of the group. Often the couple grew up together and had mutual friends. For the majority of us now, life is very different. With so much mobility, with so many young people leaving farms, towns, and small cities for large metropolitan areas, and with the general breakdown of traditional family ties, the communal spirit of marriage has been lost for millions of people. The sense of community and group sharing which has always been associated with weddings seemed to dwindle at the same rate the cities grew. The faster our society's pace, the more its essential cohesive bond —marriage—seemed to disintegrate.

Personal weddings, which began in large numbers in the 1960s, are partly a response to this situation. Couples who design their own weddings consciously choose rituals that have some meaning to them, and very often these are the festive, joyous customs of the past. The rituals of wishing luck to the couple are familiar to all of us. One of the oldest and most universal of all celebrative customs is that of throwing rice, grain, or nuts at the couple after the wedding. It is still very popular today, yet most people have no idea why they are standing around tossing Uncle Ben's Rice at good friends who were married a few minutes before.

Grains that literally sustain life also symbolically represent life and growth. A good crop is an occasion for much joy. Before our ancestors understood that babies are conceived by a man and woman in sexual intercourse, they made up stories or myths that connected pregnancy with the yearly appearance of crops. Both functions were perceived to be the same—and often blessed by the same deity. Both were very mysterious occurrences; both brought life into the world; and both involved risk and possible loss of life.

The custom of throwing rice and grain at newlyweds probably originated to symbolize the close relationship between woman and the life-bearing grain. Just as sowing seeds makes new life grow from the seeds, so might throwing grains increase the bride's fertility. Since in many cultures a barren woman could be divorced or even killed, throwing "life" in the form of grain was thought of as bringing good luck to the new wife.

Other meanings of this rite have also been recorded. Among Indians, throwing rice, the basic food source, symbolized the wish of plenty and prosperity for the couple. Nowadays this is the main sentiment involved in the custom. Throwing rice is a way of saying "Good Luck!"

But rice is not the only thing that has been thrown at weddings. In many lands eggs also represented fertility and prosperity. Westermarck notes that in Morocco, the groom throws an egg at his new wife in the hope that she will have ease in childbirth. This is a rather messy ritual, but magic is magic. In another case, dates and figs were tossed after the couple in order to make the bride sweeter to her husband. Ancient Hebrews threw barley in front of the couple to express their hopes for numerous progeny. Not just one child —five or ten! Fecundity was a blessed sign for most people until the middle of this century. Children were essential to the growth and power of a family, tribe, city, or nation. The more people, the more help available to bring in the crops or man the battle stations. A woman who could bear and raise ten children was for many centuries a hero.

In these days of great concern about the world's overpopulation, and with many couples deliberately controlling the size of their families or remaining childless, the ritual of rice throwing seems out of date to many people. On the one hand, it really expresses the wish, "Have many children." On the other hand, it would be a shame if the custom were to disappear (especially since it has lost its original meaning and now is simply another means of nonverbal celebration). Perhaps the modern meaning of rice throwing will simply be: "We wish you much happiness and prosperity."

Flowers have long been used to decorate weddings. One tradition we have inherited through the centuries is the use of "flower girls" in a wedding. One or two children may precede the bride down the aisle carrying bouquets of flowers. This is an updated version of the original ritual when children carried bunches of grain to symbolize fertility. Grains and flowers are interchangeable in this ritual because the meaning is clear: nature's "children" are used to bring luck to the humans.

In olden days, the bridal flowers were another way to represent the wish for fertility (although today many claim the bouquet is carried to hide the bride's nervously shaking hands from public view). The ritual of throwing the bouquet goes back many centuries. Numerous objects have been thrown by brides in the past —garters, cakes, wheat, or flowers—with the idea that the person who caught the object would be the next to marry. It was the bride's way of wishing luck to the unmarried girls in the crowd.

In most Jewish weddings today, the couple reenacts an ancient ritual that has all but vanished in other religions and cultures. This is the breaking of a wine glass after the bride and groom have drunk from it. The bride and groom sip the wine, then wrap the glass in a towel before the groom crushes it with his foot. This rite has been essential in Jewish services for thousands of years, but the exact meaning has apparently been lost. Some say it symbolizes man's short life on earth; that even in the midst of the happy occasion we should not forget that sorrow and death are also ahead. Other sources hark back to the significance the breaking act has had in other cultures; that is, that breaking some object is a clear sign of good luck. We are used to thinking that breaking something brings bad luck—like a mirror and its seven year omen—but in earlier times, all around the world, breaking was supposed to summon good tidings.

Most of the breaking rites witnessed at weddings symbolized the insurance of consummation in the bride. Or, to be more precise, breaking an object represented the actual loss of virginity. Breaking an object was another way of wishing the couple good luck and many children.

In India, a coconut was passed three times over the couple's heads, then broken on the ground. Here, the purpose was to drive away demons.

In several communities, a plate of salt was broken over the groom's head to insure his good luck. Salt has long been thought to have "magical" qualities—throwing salt over the left shoulder, for example, was supposed to keep the demons in check. This custom is still with us today, another superstition that has lingered on in our technological age.

In several northern European countries it was traditional to meet the new couple at the threshold of their house and break some object there. This act not only got rid of the evils in the house, but also symbolized the sexual aspect of the couple's new social position. If there is any doubt about the sexual nature of the custom, a further example will clear it up. Among peasant folk in the Slavic countries, the wedding reception was usually held in the house of the bride and groom. After a respectable amount of time with the guests, the couple retired into their bedroom to consummate the marriage. After a little while, the bride's father would throw his glass against the bedroom door. He was followed by the groom's father, and then all the other guests followed suit, tossing glasses, pots, or anything breakable. This whole scene was simply to wish the couple well and hope that intercourse would be easy and fruitful. It also indicates that sexual envy is as old as mankind! How the couple managed in the midst of this crashing sound is unknown. With such a racket going, probably they *did* need a lot of luck.

More evidence of the sexual implications of the breaking ritual can be seen in another widespread custom of crumbling a cake, then considered the wedding cake, over the head of the bride. The cakes were made of grain; so the two magical beliefs of breaking and fertility were combined to make certain the bride would conceive easily and often.

It is probably lucky for all of us that the custom of breaking everything in sight has vanished over the generations. Weddings are costly enough. With an added bill for 500 glasses and 40 windows attached to every ceremony, a couple might think twice before agreeing to a huge guest list. On the other hand, think of the fun involved in being one of the guests.

RECEPTIONS: The reception, or the feast of food, drink, and dancing, is the final public custom of weddings the world over. In virtually all societies, some kind of feast accompanies or follows the actual wedding. Wedding feasts can last only a few minutes, or as long as a week. In the Orient, for example, the drinking of wine by the bride and groom constitutes what we call the ceremony—the bond is the feast itself.

In the Western world, we expect a wedding service to be followed by a reception; it is the time to receive and acknowledge the married couple, to toast them, share in their joy, and send them on their way. But in numerous societies in the past, these two celebrations—the nuptial and the social—have been combined. People feasted with a couple as the wedding was taking place. Certainly for primitive people, the wedding *was* the feast. Only much later did the two functions become separate. We have witnessed some movement back to the "open ceremony," or extended feast, in this country recently. Couples who have combined the "wedding services" with the "reception" have tried to achieve a certain casualness and freedom in their marriage ceremony.

Eating and drinking together is one of the oldest signs of love and union. In ancient times, the bride and groom probably shared some bread and drink together and were then considered legally married. No vows, no papers to sign. It was as easy as that. By simple sharing, they were united. There are many old myths about two enemies who become friends by sharing a meal, or about a boy and girl falling in love by drinking from the same cup or goblet. When one comes this close to another, one cannot help but be affected. Jews made the drinking of wine an integral part of their marriage service. This sharing, coming together, is as universal as holding hands—it's understood by anyone in the world.

The sharing between bride and groom also extends to the guests. The communal aspect is very important. The couple, once united, share their happiness with those around them. In old times, a wedding gathering was usually made up of the entire clan, tribe, or village. A wedding day was a time for dancing and singing, often for drunkenness, and always a celebration for everyone. A wedding was truly a feast in numerous societies—laws were relaxed, people could drink openly (an act not usually condoned), and sexual mores were relaxed. In some societies, sexual intercourse was permitted even between strangers, although outlawed during normal times. And the feast wasn't always a short one; sometimes it lasted for days, or until everyone collapsed from exhaustion.

As social customs became more sophisticated and highly regulated, the wedding feast became a "reception" where the bride and groom could meet and feast with friends and relatives. The idea was the same, but the wild activities were somewhat toned down. A receiving line was formed so the couple could greet all the guests in a systematic fashion. Most of the exuberant rituals were either displaced or made acceptable to each culture. But the reception itself remained an important part of the entire wedding ritual.

Many elements of the wedding feast have not

changed since our ancestors used them. One of these is dancing. Whether to jungle drums or a rock band, a reception has never been complete without music and dancing. The dance was a central ritual in most primitive cultures, and many wedding ceremonies included ritual dances as expression of emotion. Ritual dance involves the spirits and gods, and calls them to witness and bless the occasion. Dance is a means of having everyone present participate in the celebration. And dance can also be highly erotic—another means of prayer to the gods that the couple will have ease and fruitfulness in their sexual life. Today, dancing is more a way of being social and enjoying others. Even though we no longer perform prayer dances at our friends' weddings, the enjoyment and group unity is the same as it must have been for thousands of years.

The wedding cake is another part of the feast that dates back to antiquity. The beautifully frosted, decorated, tall wedding cake we often see today is an updated version of the grain cake that was broken over the bride's head to insure fruitfulness centuries ago. The wedding cake has always been a "special" food, a mixture and shape used only for the feast. It has always been a communal food; everyone ate from it, both as a sign of union and also as a way of wishing luck to the new couple. Today many couples give each guest a small piece of their cake in boxes, to make certain everyone gets a piece to take home. This is their way of sharing their "special" moment with the community of guests.

When we see the bride and groom slicing the first piece of a huge wedding cake and offering it to each other to eat, they are enacting one of the most ancient rituals. And as all the guests join in the festivities, we can sense something very special and unique about the occasion. It is a time of joy, a time when people, many of whom do not know each other, can join together in one common interest: the wish of happiness for a newly married couple.

HONEYMOONS: A wedding isn't quite complete without a honeymoon, a time of rest and vacation for the couple. The honeymoon isn't a new idea, but the aspect of traveling away from home and family has become widespread only in the past two hundred years or so. Prior to this, the honeymoon was looked at as a short period of sexual initiation and freedom for the bride and groom. The idea of honeymoon may well have started back in primitive times when a man captured a woman from another tribe or village and then had to hide out with her for a certain time before peace could be made with her family. The aspect of getting away from everyone in order to share intimacy has always been central to the honeymoon.

The word "honeymoon" actually connoted "a month of sweetness," an interlude of happiness before returning to everyday affairs. In ancient times, a couple may have spent that time closed in their room or house, while friends and relatives took care of their meals and other necessities. Since after the advent of institutional religion sexual intercourse before marriage was strictly forbidden for women in most cultures, the new couple often barely knew one another. In countries where religion is a very strong influence and female virginity considered sacred, if a man found out that his new wife had copulated with another, he could terminate the marriage immediately, send her away, or in some cases have her put to death. Most women were careful not to let such a state of affairs occur. In other lands, notably the Slavic and Russian, consummation of the marriage by intercourse was of such importance that sometimes the best man would stand by the bed while the couple made love just to make certain all went well. As people demanded more privacy, this disconcerting custom gradually died away.

On the other hand, customs of abstaining from sexual activity for a certain time after the wedding were also widespread. This appears to contradict the importance placed on consummation, but magic and superstition were involved. Abstinence from sex was simply to keep away the dangerous spirits. In primitive times, the period of abstinence might have varied from one night to one month or more. It was believed that the couple was so vulnerable that to engage in sex and "open" the woman right away might lead to disaster. Blood from her hymen breaking was terrifying enough—but if an evil demon should enter her and defile her—then all was doomed. So the couple was required to postpone gratification.

But primitives weren't the only ones to delay the sex act. The tradition is also deeply rooted in Christian and Moslem belief, obviously a carry-over from earlier times. The tradition of "Tobias Nights" in most of the early Western world demanded three nights' abstinence to make certain the devil couldn't enter the new bride and impregnate her. Tobias was a man visited by the archangel Raphael and told to guard his wife from evil by not having sex with her for three nights. The Catholic church later modified this tradition and asked for only one night's abstention so as not to profane the benediction of the nuptial mass.

These restrictions on sexual activity seem very distant to us in these times. Sex between two people in love does not have to carry the heavy baggage of guilt or fear that it did in most societies, even up to this century. The magical superstitions and taboos that surrounded intercourse in primitive times, and the social or religious restraints of later centuries, have been scaled down to be more realistic and natural. Magical belief has faded, but the magic of sex never diminishes.

Today the honeymoon is a time for travel, relaxation, and fun. For most couples (at least those who have not lived together before marriage) it is the first time of any extended intimacy—and in this way the couple who go to a romantic spot today do not differ greatly from the couple honeymooning in their romantic spot thousands of years ago.

All of these rituals have come down to us from a wide variety of cultures and historic periods. Many of these customs are lost to us; others have been transformed, tailored to fit the cultural or religious beliefs of a particular group of people. Even though the original meaning has generally been lost in the shuffle of time and translation, the forms remain in use today. Why? Primarily because these traditions have a value in themselves, and few people thought to question what lay behind these acts until couples having personal weddings began searching, inventing, and infusing new life into the marriage ceremony. Changing weddings and rituals is an attempt to bring the past into the present, a way of saying "we're alive now, and our marriage will show it." Most of these rituals will remain alive in personal weddings. And many will gain a new interpretation and new vitality because of their having been questioned, revised, and renewed.

SELECTED READINGS

So many wedding rituals and customs have been practiced and recorded throughout the world that it would be impossible to present them all in one book. But a few anthropologists have tried to document the history and meaning of the most significant customs; the best of these books are presented below. Most of these works were written at the end of the last century or the beginning of this one; and although the prose style is often ponderous, the books contain fascinating interpretations of the rites of matrimony.

Several of the books cited at the end of "The Origins of Marriage" will be useful for reading about rituals. Westermarck's volumes are probably the most precise and interesting because they cover the most ground.

William J. Fielding's *Strange Customs of Courtship and Marriage* (Philadelphia: The Blakiston Press, 1942), is an excellent short review of most of the wedding rituals practiced in America. If you are interested in a more thorough study of rituals around the world,

Lord Avebury's *Marriage, Totemism, and Religion* (London: Longmans, Green and Company, 1911), is a good source. Others include George Carroll's *Wedding Etiquette and Uses in Polite Society* (New York: Dempsey and Carroll, 1880), a very dated and often humorous account of nuptial rituals; Lady Augusta Hamilton's *Marriage Rites, Customs, and Ceremonies of All Nations of the Universe* (London: Chapple and Son, 1882); and E. J. Wood's *The Wedding Day in All Ages and Countries* (London: Richard Bently, 1869. 2 volumes).

7
Three
Weddings

ANNE AND DAVID

Anne and David's wedding provides a good example of a church ceremony that might have been "traditional" only a few years ago. But because of the emergence of personal weddings and the many changes that have taken place in most religious organizations recently—and because of the couple's desire for a more intimate and personal service—their ceremony was unique, planned by and for themselves with their minister's help.

After David and Anne decided to get married, one of their first decisions concerned the officiant. Anne is a practicing Catholic, David is Christian but not particularly active in any denomination. They chose to look for "neutral" religious territory so their wedding would be spiritual in a way they desired, but would not impose one person's beliefs on another. Through talking with several friends, they heard of a minister who had been encouraging more personal alternatives in wedding ceremonies. David called him and made an appointment for the three of them to get together.

The first meeting was amiable. Father Rhodes is in his forties and is a forthright person. He has been active in church reform in his city since the 1960s. His parish is in an old section of town, run down and racially mixed. Much of his work has been devoted to making his church a community meeting place where everyone can congregate to discuss problems in the neighborhood. He knows that many of the old solutions to social ills are not working, that government slowness to respond to inequalities in the community is causing frustration and deep alienation.

Father Rhodes's growing distrust of pat answers to new problems spilled over to other areas as well—one of them, marriage and weddings. Having officiated at hundreds of wedding ceremonies, he was aware of the sameness, and to some extent the lifelessness, of the standard ritual. He began suggesting changes to couples years ago. At first some refused to rethink their weddings because there was no precedent—such change was somehow threatening to them. But those who met with Father Rhodes and liked his idea for altering the usual service left his office excited about the many new directions available to them. He did not dictate what *should* be done; he only suggested alternatives that a couple might want to explore—different music, the addition of dance, restructured vows, new liturgy, and so on. Father Rhodes left the decisions and the changes up to the couple. He provided ideas, not mandates.

He also changed the interior architecture of his church. Where there had once been a rectangular stone altar, Father Rhodes had a huge round platform built, elevated about a foot from the floor. On this platform he placed a simple wooden table. The arrangement enabled people to participate in religious services without being confined to the pews. Bright banners were hung around the walls to soften the bare monastic feeling of the old stone building.

When David and Anne met with Father Rhodes, they discussed the kind of atmosphere and tone their wedding would have. They talked about themselves and their feelings about getting married, what it meant to both of them, and what ideas they had for the future. Since David had been married once before, he was especially enthusiastic about a new and different ceremony for Anne and himself. He told Father Rhodes that it seemed absurd to him to repeat the same vows with another person. Anne tells of that first meeting. "I felt very good during our talk. I was a little nervous at first, but Father Rhodes isn't the kind of man you can stay nervous around for long. He was interested in hearing about *our* ideas for the wedding, not in telling us how we should feel or behave. He asked us what we thought would be the most personal way we could celebrate our wedding. Did we want a small, simple affair, or the opposite? Did we want to include everyone in the ceremony? Did we want to write our own vows? What kind of music were we partial to? He asked us a lot of things to get us thinking specifically about what direction we wanted to go in. David and I had agreed on a small wedding, but we really did not want to write the whole service. I asked Father Rhodes what he might say if we read our own vows, and he said we could choose different readings, or he would, or he could just talk informally for a short time. We discussed all the options for over an hour, and when David and I left, we knew we were going to have a beautiful wedding."

The planning didn't stop there. David and Anne decided they wanted one or two short poems read in their service. They wanted the ceremony simple and direct, so they discarded many suggestions from friends that seemed to them off-beat or wild. David said, "We didn't want a traditional ceremony, but then we didn't feel we had to break out a rock band to show everyone we're different. That wasn't the point. We simply wanted to be married in a style that was comfortable and happy for us. Just us."

At a second meeting with Father Rhodes they discussed final plans for the vows and readings, decided on a single singer with guitar for music, set the time, and cleared up other matters. Father Rhodes asked them to bring two large loaves of bread and two bottles of wine to the ceremony, "to be shared by us all."

The wedding began at eight o'clock on a Saturday night in the winter. David, Anne, the best man, and the maid of honor had arrived at the church about seven o'clock. They spoke with the guitarist who asked if they had any special pieces they wanted played; Anne had one, and the guitarist promised she would do it during the ceremony. David and Anne delivered the bread and wine to the altar table, and paced around a little nervously waiting for the guests to arrive. Instead of having the usual wedding processional, the couple waited by the front door with their parents and attendants and greeted guests as they came in.

Anne wore a colorful long dress, David a dark suit. Most of the guests wore suits or dresses, but a few had on sweaters or more casual dress.

After the guests had arrived, Anne and David moved about, talking with them. Father Rhodes appeared and joined the group for a half hour. The atmosphere was festive, and no one seemed worried about "correct timing." A little after eight o'clock, Anne told Father Rhodes that all the guests were present; he then asked everyone to join him around the platform.

About fifty friends and relatives had gathered. Father Rhodes stood in front of Anne and David and began a short talk about their marriage. "We are gathered here tonight to witness and bless David's and Anne's marriage. But we do not have the authority to sanctify this union—it comes solely from their hearts. The marriage is theirs; we are here to wish them well and give our love, understanding, and hopes to them. What is in their hearts is the only significant and true wedding of two people, yet it is our responsibility to assist and support them at all times, and as a community to cherish the love and commitment that they have for each other." Father Rhodes then went on, speaking to all the participants and the couple. He spoke informally of the religious and social aspects of the wedding, of the new responsibility David and Anne have towards each other, and about the love and friendship they share that must be carefully preserved and strengthened.

After this, he read a section of T. S. Eliot's *Four Quartets,* some verses from the Bible, and a poem by

E. E. Cummings. Then he recited the vows of matrimony, blessed the rings, and listened to David and Anne repeat the vows. Father Rhodes turned to the guests around the circle and said, "This wedding is a feast for all of us; we are party to it because we love these people and because we have witnessed their union in the eyes of God. Would anyone like to share any feelings or thoughts at this time?" After a few seconds of silence, one of Anne's cousins expressed her joy and pleasure about their marriage. Others wanted to speak, and around the circle several friends and relatives offered blessings and wishes. Many of the participants were near tears because of the emotion of the ceremony.

Father Rhodes then spoke privately with the bride and groom, and asked them to follow him to the altar table. With David's help he opened the wine bottles and poured wine into two large chalices. With Anne's help he broke the bread and placed it on a silver tray. David and Anne walked around the circle giving each guest the bread and wine to celebrate the feast. As the couple walked around, they spoke with each guest and thanked them for joining in their happiness.

The ceremony was completed. The guitarist had quietly sung spirituals through the whole service. Candles softened the glare of the few electric lights, and the church looked and felt warm, full of life. Father Rhodes blessed the couple and the guests, who gathered their coats and departed for a reception at a friend's home.

The reception, like the wedding, was simple and festive—more music, wine, and food. There were no caterers or special consultants needed. People danced and talked for hours. David and Anne cut their wedding cake (made by one of Anne's friends), fed each other a bite, and toasted their friends. The bride and groom left about one o'clock in the morning to cheers, rice, and whistles. The guests lingered a little longer.

The reception had been easily planned with the help of a few of the couple's friends. It was tasteful and relatively inexpensive considering that about fifty people were eating and drinking. Handled in another way, it might have cost thousands of dollars. Friends helped with food preparation, brought some of their favorite appetizers or main dishes, and pitched in with the kitchen chores. A bartender was hired who was able to get the champagne and liquor at a discount. The final price for food and drink was only a few hundred dollars. The emphasis was on mood and spirit, not on fanciness or extravagant extras to entertain the guests. The guests were co-celebrants in the feast with David and Anne—they did not need to be entertained as outsiders.

BETSY AND ALEX

Betsy and Alex's wedding had the appearance of a conventional Protestant ceremony. Dress was contemporary and informal; the setting was a clearing in a forest. But the text of the wedding service itself was taken primarily from the English Book of Common

Prayer, dated no later than 1602. Theirs was certainly an alternative wedding, one thought out by both partners and reflective of their interests. It was "super-traditional," as Alex said; a ceremony that was lofty in tone and promise, yet realistic and very personal, too. Instead of breaking with past traditions and rituals of their church to find alternatives for themselves, the couple reaffirmed the past more deliberately by going back to earlier texts for their vows. As Betsy suggested, they wanted to be "more married," and the vows and promises of previous centuries gave them that feeling. Alex, a Renaissance music scholar, found editions of the Book of Common Prayer from 1549, 1560, and 1602. He and Betsy lined them up together and carefully went through all the sections on matrimony, selecting prayers and vows that appealed to both of them. After they had made their selection, Alex wrote out the ceremony, retaining many of the original phrases, but modernizing some of the language.

"There were dozens of passages in the old versions that were totally unusable for us," Alex said. "The heavy emphasis on obedience and duty was something neither Betsy nor I wanted in our wedding, so we had to choose with care. But the Elizabethan language is beautiful, and, in some respects, so are the ideas people had about marriage in the sixteenth century. We reached back into the past to see what surprises were there—and we found many pleasant ones."

Alex and Betsy had little trouble in getting their minister to approve their plans. He was genuinely enthusiastic from the beginning about the rewritten ceremony and the music. The couple met with him for the first time about two months before the wedding and discussed ideas. They talked several more times before the ceremony, and on each occasion the minister expressed his excitement about their service. Like so many other officiants today, he was glad to see some new (even if old) life in the wedding ceremony.

In keeping with the tone and date of their service, the couple added a prayer and a reading from Chaucer's "The Franklin's Tale" in *Canterbury Tales*. Alex chose several pieces of Renaissance music to be played on four sackbuts, the forerunner to the trombone. The processional music (which actually went on for about thirty minutes as the guests, and then the couple, arrived), was made up of Josquin des Prez's *Una Musque de Biscaya* and *La Belle Se Siet,* and Jacob Obrecht's *Kyrie* from *Missa Sub Tuum Presidium.* During the ceremony, following the reading from Chaucer, the musicians played a few measures from the Benedictus of Obrecht's *Missa Fortuna Desparata.* The recessional music was made up of settings from Caron's *Ave Sidus Clarissimum.*

The wedding took place at noon in a small New York town about an hour's drive from Manhattan. Alex and Betsy were married in an outdoor chapel secluded in the woods, a quarter-mile from the parish church. The chapel is accessible only by foot, so the sense of privacy and remoteness was further accentuated. It was the end of May, and the woods were a bright green and wild flowers were in bloom everywhere. In the middle of the small clearing stood an altar carved out of wood and stone. Beyond the clearing was a steep hill descending to a running stream. The whole setting—primitive altar, renewed nature, and the sound of the stream heard above the music and voices—seemed both idyllic and timeless.

After the guests had assembled, Alex and his best man came down the path and waited at the altar. Then Betsy and her father entered the clearing, joining her matron of honor and the others at the altar. The minister began the service.

Dearly beloved friends, we are gathered here in the sight of God and in the face of this company, to join together this Man and this Woman in holy Matrimony; which is an honorable estate, instituted of God in Paradise, in the time of man's innocency, signifying unto us the mystical union that is betwixt Christ and His Church: which holy estate Christ adorned and beautified with His presence and first miracle that he wrought in Cana of Galilee, and is commended of Saint Paul to be honorable among all men: and therefore is not by any to be enterprised nor taken in hand unadvisedly or lightly; but reverently, discreetly, advisedly, soberly and in the fear of God, duly considering the causes for which matrimony was ordained:

One was the procreation of children, to be brought up in the fear and nurture of the Lord and praise of God. It was also ordained for the mutual society, help and comfort that the one ought to have for the other, both in prosperity and adversity: into which holy estate these two persons present come now to be joined. Therefore, if any man can show any just cause why they may not lawfully be joined together, let him speak now, or else hereafter for ever hold his peace.

¶ And also speaking unto the Persons who are to be married, he shall say,

I require and charge you, (as you will answer at the dreadful day of judgment, when the secrets of all hearts shall be disclosed) that if either of you do know any impediment, why you may not be lawfully joined together in Matrimony, that ye confess it. For be ye well assured, that so many as be coupled together, otherwise than God's word doth allow, are not joined of God, neither is their marriage lawful.

¶ If no impediment is alleged, then shall the Minister say unto the Man,

Alexander, wilt thou have this Woman to thy wedded wife, to live together after God's ordinance in the holy estate of Matrimony? Wilt thou love her, comfort her, honor and keep her, in sickness and in health? And forsaking all other, keep thee only to her, so long as ye both shall live?

¶ The Man shall answer,

I will.

¶ Then shall the Minister say unto the Woman,

Elizabeth, wilt thou have this Man to thy wedded husband, to live together after God's ordinance, in the holy estate of Matrimony? Wilt thou obey him, and serve him, love, honor, and keep him, in sickness and in health? And forsaking all other, keep thee only to him, so long as ye both shall live?

¶ The Woman shall answer

I will.

¶ Then the Minister shall say,

Who giveth this Woman to be married unto this Man?

¶ And the Minister receiving the woman at her father's hands shall cause the Man to take the Woman by the right hand and so either to give their troth to the other, the Man first saying,

I, Alexander, take thee Elizabeth to my wedded wife, to have and to hold, from this day forward, for better, for worse, for richer, for poorer, in sickness and in health, to love and to cherish, till death us depart: according to God's holy ordinance, and thereto I plight thee my troth.

¶ Then shall they loose their hands and the Woman taking again the Man by the right hand, shall say,

I, Elizabeth, take thee Alexander to my wedded husband, to have and to hold, from this day forward, for better, for worse, for richer, for poorer, in sickness and in health, to love and to cherish, till death us depart, according to God's holy ordinance: and thereto I give thee my troth.

¶ Then shall they again loose their hands, and the Man shall give unto the Woman a Ring on this wise: the Minister taking the Ring shall deliver it unto the Man, to put it upon the fourth finger of the Woman's left hand. And the Man holding the Ring there, and taught by the Minister, shall say,

With this ring I thee wed: with my body I thee worship: and with all my worldly goods I thee endow. In the name of the Father, and of the Son, and of the holy Ghost. Amen.

¶ Then the Minister shall say,

Bless, O Lord, this Ring, that he who gives it and she who wears it may abide in thy peace, and continue in thy favor, unto their life's end; through Jesus Christ our Lord. Amen.

¶ Then shall they again loose their hands, and the Woman shall give unto the Man a Ring as above, and the Woman, holding the Ring on the Man's hand, and taught by the Minister, shall say,

With this ring I thee wed: with my body I thee worship: and with all my worldly goods I thee endow. In the name of the Father, and of the Son, and of the holy Ghost. Amen.

¶ Then the Minister shall say,

Bless, O Lord, this Ring, that she who gives it and he who wears it may abide in thy peace and continue in thy favor, unto their life's end; through Jesus Christ our Lord. Amen.

¶ Then the Minister shall say,

Let us pray.

O eternal God, creator and preserver of all mankind, giver of all spiritual grace, the author of everlasting life: send thy blessing upon these servants, this Man and this Woman, whom we bless in thy name, that as Isaac and Rebecca lived faithfully together: so these persons may surely perform and keep the vow and covenant betwixt them made, whereof this Ring given, and this, and received, are tokens and pledges. And may ever remain in perfect love and peace together: and live according to thy laws: through Jesus Christ our Lord. Amen.

¶ Then the Minister shall add,

O almighty God, Creator, who only art the well-spring of life; Bestow upon these servants, if it be thy will, the gift and heritage of children; and grant that they may see their children brought up in thy faith and fear, to the honor and glory of thy name; through Jesus Christ our Lord. Amen.

¶ Then shall the Minister join their right hands together, and say,

Those whom God hath joined together, let no man put asunder.

At this point in the ceremony, a friend of the groom read the following passage from Chaucer's "The Franklin's Tale":

For there is one thing I can safely say: that those bound by love must obey each other if they are to keep company long. Love will not be constrained by mastery; when mastery comes, the God of love at once beats his wings, and farewell—he is gone. Love is a thing as free as any spirit; women naturally desire liberty, and not to be constrained like slaves; and so do men, if I shall tell the truth. See who is the most patient in love: he has the greatest advantage. Patience is surely a great virtue, for it vanquished, as these scholars say, things that rigor would never manage. One cannot scold or complain at every word. Learn to endure patiently, or else, as I live and breathe, you shall learn it whether you want or not. For certainly there is no one in this world who doesn't do or say something amiss. Anger, sickness, or planetary influences, wine, sorrow, or changing of disposition often causes one to do or speak amiss. A man cannot be avenged for every wrong; according to the occasion, everyone who knows how must use temperance. And therefore a wise man, in order to live in comfort, promises his lady forbearance, and she wisely gives her promise to him that there be no fault in her.

Then the Prayer Book ceremony continued, the minister saying to the people:

For as much as Elizabeth and Alexander have consented together in holy wedlock, and have witnessed the same here before God and this company, and thereto have given and pledged their troth either to the other, and have declared the same by giving and receiving rings, and by joining of hands: I pronounce that they are Man and Wife, in the name of the Father, and of the Son, and of the holy Ghost. Amen.

¶ And the Minister shall add this blessing,

God the Father bless you. God the Son keep you. God the holy Ghost lighten your understanding. The Lord mercifully with his favor look upon you, and so fill you with all spiritual benediction and grace, that you may have remission of your sins in this life and in the world to come, life everlasting. Amen.

¶ The Man and the Woman shall kneel afore the altar, and the Minister standing at the altar, and turning his face toward them, shall say,

Our Father, who art in heaven, etc., And lead us not into temptation.

¶ Answer,

But deliver us from evil. Amen.

¶ Then the Minister shall say,

O merciful Lord, and heavenly Father, by whose

gracious gift mankind is increased, we beseech thee, assist with thy blessing these two persons, that they may both be fruitful in procreation of children, and also live together so long in godly love and honesty, that they may see their children's children, unto the third and fourth generation, unto thy praise and honor: through Jesus Christ our Lord. Amen.

O God, who by thy mighty power hast made all things of nought; who also after other things set in order, didst appoint that out of man woman should take her beginning, and knitting them together, didst teach that it should never be lawful to put asunder those whom thou by Matrimony hadst made one: O God, who hadst consecrated the state of Matrimony to such an excellent mystery, that in it is signified and represented the spiritual marriage and unity betwixt Christ and his Church; look mercifully upon these thy servants, that both this Man may love his wife, according to thy word, and also that this Woman may be loving and amiable to her husband as Rachel, wise as Rebecca, faithful and obedient as Sara, and in all quietness, sobriety, and peace, be a follower of holy and godly matrons. O Lord, bless them both, and grant them to inherit thy everlasting kingdom, through Jesus Christ our Lord. Amen.

Almighty God, who at the beginning did create our first parents, Adam and Eve, and did sanctify and join them together in marriage, pour upon you the riches of His grace, sanctify and bless you, that ye may please Him both in body and soul: and live together in holy love, unto your lives' end. Amen.

Their ceremony over, the couple kissed and then walked up the path to the cadence of the sackbut music. The effect of the wedding was surprising. It was a formal and elegant ceremony because of the language, yet in the outdoor setting the tone seemed very natural, too. And even though much of the ceremony was hundreds of years old, Alex's and Betsy's changes and additions gave the service a new and personal feeling.

The reception was held in Betsy's parents' garden, complete with tents and canopied areas. Food and service were catered, so a sit-down luncheon for the hundred guests was not a huge problem. The couple made a compromise with the bride's parents before the wedding: Betsy and Alex could have their wedding ceremony as they wanted if Betsy's mother could plan the reception. Since this is what she did as a profession, it seemed only right. They went along with the arrangement and it turned out happily for everyone.

The main entertainment of the afternoon continued to be music—and dancing. Many of the guests played instruments, a soloist sang several pieces, there were many duets, and another group performed a fourteenth-century piece on recorders. In the middle of the reception, everyone gathered to sing "Amazing Grace," followed by several Southern gospel songs.

After the luncheon and the cutting of the wedding cake (and many toasts), Alex and Betsy left on their honeymoon. Guests lingered for a short time and then departed. It had been a long, festive day. And the wedding ceremony, 1602 style, seemed very appropriate, even in the 1970s.

BARB AND HOWIE

Barb and Howie celebrated their marriage on a winter evening in the living room of their new home in Minneapolis. The ceremony was planned by them, with the complete approval of their minister. Like many alternative weddings today, it combined rituals, poems, songs, and customs from a variety of cultures and religions, and the mixture was appropriate. Howie is Jewish by birth, and Barb is a Lutheran. The minister who officiated was born a Jew and is now a Unitarian.

About twenty-five guests were invited. They were met at the door by Howie's six-year-old niece and nephew who gave each person a flower. Barb's brother handed out programs which included the text for a reading during the ceremony. A friend was playing the piano in the hall. People mingled and talked with friends they had not seen for some time. Many of the guests had come from out of town, so a few brief introductions were made. Howie and Barb greeted everyone and expressed their pleasure that each could come.

When everyone had arrived and had warmed up from the cold, Howie asked the guests to find a seat in the living room. Chairs and couches had been set up in a large circle, and as the people got settled, Howie turned out the lights in all the rooms and, with the help of others, lit the twenty candles that were placed around the living room. The room glowed in the flickering candlelight, and soon everyone fell silent.

The wedding began as Howie took his seat. Barb was standing at the top of the stairs, holding a bouquet of daisies in her hands. Howie's young niece and nephew stood on the step below her, also holding flowers. Howie looked up toward Barb; accompanying himself on a guitar, he began to sing a song adapted from "Wanderlove" by Mason Williams.

> Come my love and we shall wander
> All of life to see and know.
> In our journey's lost wood rambling,
> Seasons come and seasons go.

From the stairs, Barb sang:

> Come my love and we shall wander,
> Just to see what we can find.
> If we only find each other,
> Still the journey's worth the time.

As the bride and the two children descended, Barb and Howie sang the first verse again, together. Howie met Barb at the circle, and they walked over to their seats, still singing.

Bob, the minister who officiated, said, "This is a day that the Lord has made. Let us rejoice and be glad in it." He turned toward Barb, and with a gesture and smile, encouraged her to begin. "It is a very precious thing to have all these people we love so much together at one time," she said. "Since many of you do not know each other, Howie and I want to start our wedding by introducing everyone and saying a few things about each person."

Looking to her left, Barb said, "This is Gretchen, my old friend and roommate from college. We've been through a lot together—laughing and crying, singing and sharing. She's one of my closest friends, and I couldn't imagine her not being here to share this tonight."

It was Howie's turn next. "To Gretchen's left are my Mom and Dad. I guess if I have the ability to make this marriage work—through giving and through loving—it comes as a result of the giving and the loving that I have received from them.

"Next are Sid and Marianne. They have been very important people to me as I developed a sense of who I am and what I want to do with my life. We've been friends for many years, and we've done more working and playing together than I can remember.

"Behind Marianne is Rob. We've known each other since we were four years old, and I really grew up as a member of his family as well as my own. Our friendship goes back a long way, and we've spent quite a bit of time together in different struggles and causes over the years. It's really a pleasure that you're here, Rob."

After Howie had introduced a few more people, Barb spoke. "Next is my little brother Chip. I delight in calling him that because he's about six feet five inches tall, and I have a great time teasing him. He's my oldest playmate, and my oldest friend, too."

As Howie and Barb proceeded around the room introducing each person, the mood of the wedding seemed to be both attentive and relaxed. During the period of planning, Barb and Howie had realized that one of the most important things to both of them was that everyone should get to know each other and participate in the ceremony as a group. By telling everyone a little about each friend or relative, Barb and Howie helped bring the group together. By the time the introductions and funny anecdotes or stories were completed, every guest in the room felt that they knew something important about everyone else. Several times someone would interrupt Barb or Howie to set them straight on a reminiscence. The dialogue usually sent the whole company into laughter.

Yet the experience was also very serious. Barb and Howie were talking about people they loved and had deep feeling for, people who had gathered for this important event in their lives. The mixture of gaiety and seriousness was very appropriate in their wedding.

When Barb and Howie had finished going around the circle, there was silence in the room for a few moments. Everyone seemed to be thinking about what the couple had said about each guest and how it all related to their wedding. The value placed on a communal spirit was evident. Then the minister spoke. "It's right that all of you are gathered here. You're the people who know and love Barb and Howie the best, and the ones they know and love the best. It's in part because of all of you that they have become the particular people that they are. The ideas, ideals, hopes, preconceptions, and expectations that they bring to this shared life of theirs are, in some part, of your making. You are all involved in their marriage. You're party to it, so it's appropriate that you take part in it. We would like to take this time for you to share any thoughts or feelings you have with Barb and Howie and with the whole community. Feel free to say, or read, or sing, or play whatever you would like to express."

Almost everyone in the room had something to say. It was a free-wheeling variety of old remembrances, hopes for the future, humorous advice, and very serious statements of love for the couple. Some people read poems, some sang special songs; but most of the participants spoke what they were feeling at the time. Barb's mother and Chip both expressed their joy for her and Howie, but also said that they would miss her when she moved away. The emotions of happiness and some sorrow came across in both of their statements, and everyone in the room was deeply touched by the honesty and love that was so clearly felt.

Howie's father spoke of some of the traditions in their family that he hoped Howie would carry out. One was loving his in-laws and getting close to another family. "Another tradition which was started by my father, with respect to weddings, is this: when a young man of the family would bring home his prospective bride to my father and inquire, 'Well, Pop, what do you think? How do you like her?' he would say, and I'll answer the same way my father did: 'I wish you were the father and I were the son.' " Everyone in the room exploded in laughter.

When it was apparent that those who wished to speak had done so, the minister spoke again. "Why does every society we know of—every tribe, community, nation—have some sort of formal observance, some ceremonial, on the occasion of marriage?

"Perhaps because marriage is a major crossing in

life, a significant change in the state of the world; and men and women find it important to recognize such changes, to celebrate them, and to convey to the people affected and to the surrounding community the nature of the change that is taking place.

"But marriage is a very personal kind of change in the state of the world. Every marriage is the singular handiwork of two unique people. And so every marriage is different from all others. That is why this ceremony this evening is different from all others. Barb and Howie have tried, in planning their wedding, to create an observance that might truly express what *their* marriage is to be. And there is no more fitting way to symbolize a loving life together than to express that uniqueness and that love in this ceremony.

"Barb and Howie, you know best of all the nature of your own marriage, the character of your commitment to each other. Will you share some of your feelings and thoughts with each other and with this community?"

Barb thought for a moment, then turned toward Howie and began. "I remember a time not too long ago when I said to you, 'Howie, wouldn't you be better off not considering my plans or needs, but rather staying with your own plans and leaving me out of the picture?' And you asked me the same question. Our answers were very similar. For me it was a feeling that above all, I wanted to be with you, to be part of your life. It was more than just an intellectual understanding; it was more than knowing that we both have many common interests. It was something deep inside of me affirming the choices that I'm now making in my life

. . . a very rich knowing that we both wanted to build a life together, and that was most important of all.

"I hope that we can continue to maintain the kind of communication that is based on the honest sharing of our own thoughts and feelings; that it will be a relationship in which there's trust and openness. I know we can help each other grow and learn, and I hope we can do the same for others, too. I commit myself to this type of relationship and its changing process in the hope that we can continue to nourish our living and our loving."

Barb reached behind her for a guitar and sang to Howie Buffy Sainte-Marie's "Wedding Song."

> And my smile will know your joy, my love
> And my eyes will know your tears.
> And your name through my heart will throb,
> And your life through my years.
>   And my lips will know your song, my love,
>   And your hands will know my fire,
>   And my need in your strength will dwell,
>   And my sleep within your sigh.
> And my pain will know your secrets
> And my trust will know your plan.
> And your silence fill my empty hours,
> And my heart will understand.

After she had finished her song, there was silence for a moment, and then Howie, looking directly at Barb, said, "When we first met, I had the feeling that you were such an alive and exciting person, with integrity and direction of your own, that I had a sense of fear of trying to link our lives together. Fear of deterring you from your own direction, and the same for myself. And one of my biggest commitments in this marriage is to do whatever I can to help you find what you want to do, and be who you want to be. And I hope that I can go with you in those directions, and that you'll do the same with me."

Howie spoke more about the commitment he felt to Barb, and also his commitment to making society more open and livable for everyone. "I don't see that social commitment as being entirely separate from our personal one. You and I have talked a great deal about wanting our lives to have some effect that's greater than just our own close circle. I feel that this is a real goal for us, and a big part of our marriage.

"To express the more personal commitment, I've changed some of the words of a song we both know, to say some things that I hope and feel about our marriage.

> The water is wide,
> I cannot cross over,
> And neither have I wings to fly.
> Let's build a boat that can carry two,
> And both shall row, my love and I.
>
> My love is old, my love is young,
> Whether she's sad or filled with fun.
> My love is wise beyond her years,
> My love is strong beneath her fears.

We'll travel the world, my love and I,
'Long rocky shores, o'er mountains high.
We'll taste each moment, live each day,
True to each self, we'll make our way.

Oh love is handsome, and love is fine,
Bright as a jewel when first it is new.
I'll try in every way I know
To nurture it and help it grow.

And however we shall part
And one more time in life must start,
Let it be remembered through the tears
The warmth and fullness of our years.

The water is wide, I cannot cross over,
And neither have I wings to fly.
Let's build a boat that can carry two,
And both shall row, my love and I.

Howie finished his song and the room fell silent again. Everyone was caught up in the statements that the bride and groom had made to each other. The things they said were not read from a script, but came from their immediate feelings.

Then the minister spoke again. "What makes two people decide to go through the ritual of formal marriage? They love each other already; their lives are already linked. What is changed by this ceremonial?

"Really nothing at all. The ceremony doesn't change anything significantly. Its importance is only as a sign, a showing forth, of a change that has already come about in the hearts and lives of two people.

"As a community, we have witnessed the expression of care, respect, and love that has developed between Barb and Howie. As they exist as partners in their own eyes, now let them exist as partners in all of our eyes. It is not we who pronounce them husband and wife, for the true meaning of those words for them is known only to them. Instead, let us acknowledge the bond which exists between them. Let us recognize and rejoice that Barb and Howie are as truly married as two human beings can be. Each is a separate and growing person, yet each is committed to share in the other's growth and also to encourage it. Let us join our voices together and affirm Barb and Howie in the path they have chosen for themselves."

The guests reached for their programs and, following Bob, began to read from the community reading. "We ask for them the excitement of new discoveries and new creations, that their lives may be an adventure together wherever they go.

"We know that love is not easily achieved. We ask that they find the courage and the patience to overcome any obstacles, to maintain a profound communication—the very cornerstone of all relationships.

"We recognize that love is not limited and cannot be contained. We ask that love extend to their relationships with all people, and to the world in which they live.

"We dedicate ourselves to the continuing process of helping them to let their love so shine that it touches all who know them; and may their lives be lived for themselves and all mankind."

Barb and Howie each took a wine glass from a table behind them. As Bob filled their glasses with wine, he repeated the Hebrew blessing:

> Baruch atah Adonai, Elohaynu
> Melech ha-olam, boray
> p'ri ha-gafen.

Blessed art Thou, O Lord, our God, King of the
    Universe,
Who bringeth forth the fruit of the vine.

As one of the guests began to play her guitar and sing "Sunrise, Sunset," the bride and groom each held their glass up to the other to sip. Then they moved around the circle, offering each person the glass to drink from. They moved slowly, saying a few words quietly to each guest. All the time the song could be heard.

> Is this the little girl I carried?
> Is this the little boy at play?
> I don't remember growing older,
> When did they?
>
> When did she get to be a beauty,
> When did he grow to be so tall?
> Wasn't it yesterday
> When they were small?
>
> Sunrise, sunset, sunrise, sunset,
> Swiftly flow the days.

Seedlings turn overnight to sunflowers,
Blossoming even as we gaze.

Sunrise, sunset, sunrise, sunset,
Swiftly fly the years.
One season following another,
Laden with happiness and tears.

Now is the little boy a bridegroom.
Now is the little girl a bride.
Under the canopy I see them,
Side by side.

By now Barb and Howie had completed the circle and moved in front of the fireplace. As the singer sang the next verse, Howie placed the wedding ring on Barb's finger.

Place the gold ring around her finger.
Share the sweet wine and break the glass.
Soon the full circle
Will have come to pass.

As they waited for the song to end, they stood looking at each other. Then they turned to the group, gave the Hebrew toast "L'Chayim" ("To Life!"), drank the wine in their glasses, and then smashed them in the fireplace.

As they joined hands and walked back to their seats, they chanted a Navajo song:

Hey-ney-a-na, hey-hey-a-na
Hey-ney-a-na, hey-a-hey-yo,
Hey-a-hey-ey-yo.

We walk in beauty, yes we do, yes we do,
We talk in beauty, yes we do, yes we do,
We sing of beauty, yes we do,
For all of you,
Hey-a-hey-ya-hey-ya-hey-yo.

With Barb and Howie seated again before him, Bob offered the benediction—a creation myth of the Ewe speaking tribes of Togo, West Africa:

" 'In the beginning, God made a man and a woman and set them on the earth. The two looked at each other and burst out laughing. Then they traveled the earth together.'

"Barb and Howie, go in peace.

"Everyone, shalom."

Afterword and Acknowledgments

THIS BOOK COULD NOT have been written without the generous help of many friends throughout the country. Hundreds of people shared their thoughts and experiences with us. They sent programs, invitations, pictures, prayers, vows, readings, and other material used in their personal weddings. Many of them went out of their way to get in touch with others who had had personal weddings—and in this way, our information kept growing. Many others took time to write detailed accounts of their own, or friends', weddings. Still others consented to long interviews and answering our questionnaire.

Those who learned of the book were excited by the possibility of sharing their experiences. They wanted to help encourage other couples to achieve the same satisfaction they had experienced in planning, and realizing, their own weddings.

Although it is impossible to list the names of all the people who helped us, we want to give a special thanks to the ones mentioned here. In many ways, these people, friends and strangers, are the real authors of *The Wedding Book*.

Susan and Barry Strahm

Lawrence and Virginia Duncan

Helen and Michael Gabria, Jr.

Nancy VanDerwater

Rev. and Mrs. John W. Watson

Bill Thompson

Sharon and Steven Babbitt

Carl Haynes

Dennis Stratton

Larry and Ronnie Konner

Liliane Lazar

Jana Carter

Al Stiller

Ed and Linda Finn

Father John Seiler

Elaine Walker Donges

Kathy Kreis

Cris Meriam

Leonard Golen

Lee Slimmon

Wayne Kliman

Barbara Nagle

Mary Hodgson

Gary Martin

Ken Kaminsky

Barbara Glaser

Marie Smith

Pam and Jim Folk

Sue Gurian

Brad Stocker

Maxine Kamin

Carl Bovee

Lee Ann Duggan

Gretchen Clemence

Chris and Bill Dettmann

Carol Marshall

Susan and Charles Kubat

Karen and Tony Barone

Sister Claudette Schiratti

Dorothy McEvoy

Linda and Robert Schoffel

Neil Tift

Gene and Cathie Fisher

Penelope Bernard

John and Pat Gottfried

Alex and Betsy Blachly

William and Susan Lemos

Anne Harrison

Carole Scherer

Mary and Michael Lewis

Dale and Frank Hill

Elaine Allen Tift

Diane Churchill

Michael Kramer

Archie and Jeanne Givens

Maria Leonard

Fred DeRoche

Tyler Bishop

Kent and Donna Dannen
Rev. Jamie Forrest
Rev. Howard Hannon
Rev. Jim Freda
Jane and John Mooty
Elizabeth Zayatz

Dena Seiden
Ed and Jan Hecht
Rev. Robert Lehman
David and Katy True
James and Thelma
   Murphy

ACKNOWLEDGMENTS

Grateful acknowledgment is made to the following publishers and agents for permission to use copyrighted materials from the sources listed:

Howard A. Doyle Publishing Company—*Individuality and Encounter* by Clark Moustakas.

Real People Press—*Notes to Myself* by Hugh Prather.

Harper & Row, Publishers, Inc.—"Marriage" by Edward Carpenter from *That Tremendous Love*, edited by Fulton J. Sheen. Copyright © 1967 by Fulton J. Sheen. Used by permission of the publisher.

Harcourt, Brace, Jovanovich, Inc. and MacGibbon & Kee Ltd—"i thank You God for most this amazing" copyright 1950 by E. E. Cummings; "if everything happens that can't be done" copyright 1944 by E. E. Cummings, renewed 1972 by Nancy Andrews; "somewhere i have never travelled,gladly beyond" copyright 1931, renewed 1959 by E. E. Cummings. All three poems reprinted from *Complete Poems 1913–1962* by E. E. Cummings. Used by permission of the publishers.

Abingdon Press—*Inscape* by Ross Snyder.

Lawrence & Wishart Ltd.—*Aeschylus and Athens* by George Thomson.

Alfred A. Knopf, Inc.—*The Prophet* by Kahlil Gibran.

Alfred A. Knopf, Inc. and Faber and Faber Ltd.—*Markings* by Dag Hammarskjold, translated by Sjoberg and Auden.

Time, The Weekly Newsmagazine—"I Take Thee, Baby" Copyright by Time, Inc. Used by permission.

Business Week—"New Brides Ring Out the Old Tradition" Copyright © 1971 by McGraw-Hill, Inc.

Lexicon Music, Inc.—"Pass It On" by Kurt Kaiser. Copyright © 1969 by Lexicon Music, Inc. Used by permission.

Irving Music, Inc.—"Wanderlove" Words and music by Mason Williams. Copyright © 1967 by Irving Music, Inc. (BMI) All rights reserved. Used by permission.

Miller Music Corp.—"Today" Words and music by Randy Sparks. Copyright © 1964 by Metro-Goldwyn-Mayer Inc. Rights controlled by

Miller Music Corp. by arrangement with Heritage House. Used by permission.

Sunbeam Music, Inc.—"Sunrise, Sunset" by Sheldon Harnick and Jerry Bock. Copyright © 1964 by Sunbeam Music, Inc., 1700 Broadway, New York, New York 10019. International copyright secured. All rights reserved.

Gypsy Boy Music, Inc.—"The Wedding Song" by Buffy Sainte-Marie. Copyright © 1967 Gypsy Boy Music, Inc. Printed with permission of the publisher.